9·9·76

BUDDHISTS FIND CHRIST

BUDDHISTS FIND CHRIST

The Spiritual Quest of Thirteen Men and Women

in

BURMA CHINA JAPAN KOREA SRI LANKA THAILAND VIETNAM

Compiled and edited by Patrick O'Connor

of the Society of St. Columban

CHARLES E. TUTTLE COMPANY
Rutland, Vermont and Tokyo, Japan

REPRESENTATIVES

Continental Europe:
BOXERBOOKS, INC., Zurich

British Isles:
PRENTICE-HALL INTERNATIONAL, INC.,
London

Canada:
HURTIG PUBLISHERS, Edmonton

Australasia:
PAUL FLESCH & CO., PTY. LTD.
c/o BOOKWISE AUSTRALIA
104 Sussex Street, Sydney

Published by the Charles E. Tuttle Company, Inc.
of Rutland, Vermont & Tokyo, Japan
with editorial offices at
Suido 1-chome, 2-6, Bunkyo-ku, Tokyo

1933136

TABLE OF CONTENTS

1933136

TABLE OF CONTENTS

v

INTRODUCTION

In the following pages one sees some twentieth-century Asians facing the great question of human destiny. Their narratives, simple and intensely sincere, show them seeking spiritual enlightenment in a period of widespread cultural, social and political change.

As practising Buddhists and as seekers, they felt the impact of ideas old and new. Mindful of the sound values in Buddhist ethics, they were sensitive to other influences, too. Among these were ancestral tradition, nationalist sentiment, the modern scientific mentality, persistent hunger of heart and soul, and—gradually perceived—the credentials of Christianity.

Every man, every woman encounters Jesus Christ at some time, distinctly or indistinctly, if only by hearing of Him and of His Church. But everybody does not "find" Him in the full sense of accepting Him and all that He offers.

This book contains the stories of some who have found Him. They have attached themselves to Him because in Him they have found truth and grace and peace of soul. Those whose narratives are given here are only a few out of multitudes. The great majority of Christians in Asia and throughout the world are unused to writing for publication. Many would hesitate, for personal or family reasons, to tell their story in print. Those whose accounts appear in this book wrote only in response to my earnest request.

Every such story, written or unwritten, is unique, because every human person is a separate individual, though a member of a vast community. The steps by which one person comes to accept Christ are never exactly the same as those taken by another. All, however, converge and lead to One Lord, One Faith, One Baptism.

The good and true elements in Buddhism are not lost when a Buddhist finds Christ. Rather, they are preserved, developed and enhanced in spiritual value.

Christ Himself described His mission to all mankind and to every individual in these words:

> "I have come that they may have life and may have it more abundantly. I am the Good Shepherd. The Good Shepherd gives His life for His sheep."[1]

Those who have found Christ can tell that He brings to full flower all that is right and true in the creeds and practices of sincere men and women. To truth He adds a wider truth. He fortifies sincerity with abundant spiritual help.

For the writers of this book the finding they narrate is only the beginning of a story destined to reach its climax in the everlasting joys of Heaven.

P. O'C.

St. Columban's, Tokyo

---

[1] St. John's Gospel, X, 10-11.

BUDDHISTS ON BUDDHISM

by Patrick O'Connor

(The following does not pretend to be an exposition of Buddhist doctrine. It is mainly a report of some informal conversations in which qualified spokesmen answered questions about important aspects of Buddhism.)

"Buddhism is not a religion, as religion is understood in the Orient and the West. Nor is it a philosophy. What is called Buddhist philosophy is only a philosophical explanation of the Buddha's doctrine."

So spoke Thich Minh Chau, one of the most scholarly Buddhists in Vietnam. Born in 1920, he has done higher studies in Buddhist manuscripts in the Nalenda Pali Research Institute affiliated with the University of Bihar, India. He is now president of the Buddhist Van Hanh University in Saigon. As his title "Thich," used for Buddhist clergy, indicates, he is a bonze or monk.

Belief in God is not Buddhist doctrine. "We do not deny or affirm the existence of God," Thich Minh Chau said.

I reminded him that Christians and Buddhists alike believe that good deeds bring reward and evil deeds bring punishment. This is a law that both creeds recognize. Who, in the Buddhist view, is the law-maker?

"Nobody made the law," he answered. "It is nature—natural law."

"But somebody must have made 'nature.'"

1

"Nobody makes nature," he said. "It is a natural process of different elements or energies."

A senior bonze of another pagoda, Thich Minh Truc, president of the General Buddhist Association in South Vietnam, told me:

"Buddha never spoke of God, never spoke of an absolute Creator. The universe is formed by the elements."

I asked him who, in his opinion, made the law of recompense for good and bad actions. He held that there is no law or legislator. There are only causes and effects, he said, and no lawmaker has decreed what kind of effect would follow an act.

A leading lay Buddhist scholar, Mai Tho Truyen, spoke to me of divine mercy, compassion and love. But he would not agree that this implied a Divine Being who is merciful, compassionate and loving.

While the educated Buddhist may be agnostic or atheistic, it seems that the general body of Buddhists tend to believe in a Supreme Being. Thich Minh Chau would agree that many of the ordinary faithful deify Buddha himself, though he never claimed to be any more than an enlightened teacher.

Still exploring for common ground, I reminded Thich Minh Chau that Christians and Buddhists both believe that physical death is not the end of man's existence, that there is an after-life. But, I asked, does Buddhism teach that it is the same personality that survives after physical death?

Here we encountered the Buddhist doctrine of rebirth[1] into other beings, human or animal.

"It is the same person and not the same," the bonze replied. "It is the same in that he brings along with him an inheritance from his past deeds. It is not the same because when he is born, he is subject to the influence of his surroundings and so he receives new influences when he is born again."

The founder of Buddhism, the Indian prince Gautama, who lived in the sixth century before Christ, left his wife and child to seek liberation from suffering. After five years of meditation he received his "Enlightenment" by which he concluded that all pain and suffering arise from desires. He taught a code of self-mastery, including deeds of compassion, by which human desires would be gradually extinguished. The ultimate goal would be a state[2] in which extinction of craving and desires had been achieved.

Prince Gautama was given the title "Buddha," meaning the Enlightened One. He founded no church. The only community traceable to early Buddhism is the *Sangha* or community of monks living according to the code in a temple or pagoda. There is no contemporary or near-contemporary record of Buddha's life and teaching. His followers refer to him as the Lord Buddha. His statue, showing him sitting in meditation, is venerated in every Buddhist temple and in many Buddhist homes.

There are many divisions of Buddhism. The two main divisions, inside which many sects exist, are the *Theravada* and the *Mahayana*. The latter name means "Greater Vehicle," and among those who belong to this school the *Theravada* system is often called *Hinayana* or "Lesser Vehicle" in a somewhat disparaging sense. The *Theravada* Buddhists are found mainly in South-East Asia from Burma and Sri Lanka (Ceylon) through the southern delta of Vietnam as far as Saigon. The *Mahayana* followers are in Saigon and north of it, all the way to Japan.

Theravada Buddhism is regarded as closer to the original forms, while *Mahayana* is a broader and more elastic version. Both kinds have strictly observant members, some of whom never eat meat or drink wine. The usual garb of the Theravada bonze or monk is yellow, worn with one shoulder bare. The robe most commonly worn by *Mahayana* bonzes is brown.[3]

Notes

BUDDHISTS ON BUDDHISM

[1] I had written "transmigration of souls," but Dr. Thich Minh Chau preferred the word "rebirth."

[2] i.e. *Nirvana,* from a Sanskrit word meaning "a blowing out." In Buddhism it signifies "the extinction of the fire of passion in one who attains release. Whether such a person becomes extinct at death is classed... among the questions which the Buddha refused to answer" — Encyclop. Brit., Vol. XVI, art. Nirvana.

[3] This chapter was submitted to Dr. Thich Minh Chau for criticism. He found that only what he termed "some slight alterations" were called for, and these I have made. He was kind enough to say that the article expressed his thought better than anything he had seen in a long time. I am grateful to this distinguished Buddhist scholar for his courtesy and helpfulness.

INTRODUCING . . .

Thirteen citizens of Asian countries whose quest for the spiritual enlightenment sought by Buddhists has led them to Christ. The countries represented by the writers are Burma, Thailand, Sri Lanka (Ceylon), Vietnam, China, Korea and Japan.

The personal histories in this book show how the writers, as Buddhists and in their spiritual quest, felt the force of influences old and new, such as family loyalty, nationalism, the modern scientific mentality and persistent hunger of heart and soul. In such experiences they are typical of innumerable twentieth-century Asians, for whom — as for others around the world—light and encouragement may be found in these pages.

BETTER THAN MONEY COULD BUY

by Dr. Lert Srichandra

Lert Srichandra, born in Bangkok, was a Thai Buddhist. At the age of twenty-one he duly entered the Buddhist priesthood for three months during the Buddhist Lenten period.

Subsequently he entered the Jesuits' Wah Yan College, Hong Kong, and studied there for three years under the guidance of Rev. Daniel Donnelly, S.J. He was baptized, taking the name of Sebastian Conrad, in Hong Kong Cathedral.

He went to Ireland and entered University College, Dublin (National University of Ireland), and was qualified as a medical doctor with degrees of M.B., B.Ch., B.A.O., L.M. He also took a course in theological study and was awarded a certificate of honor.

Before returning to Bangkok, Thailand, in 1942, he married in University Church, Dublin, Jean Hu-Wasson, daughter of Rev. and Mrs. J. S. Wasson of the Presbyterian Church. She became a Catholic.

With the approval of H.E. Bishop Louis Chorin of Bangkok, Thailand, he founded the Catholic Association of Thailand and was its President for four years. He also was one of the founders of St. Joseph's Hospital and the Catholic Centre of Bangkok.

DEDICATION

To those who sow the seed by the wayside,

To those who sow the seed among the thorns,

To those who sow the seed upon the rock,

To those who sow the seed upon good ground. . .

Each and every one of these sowers knowingly and unknowingly, in his own way, has led me step by step until my soul has found its Creator.

God bless them all.

* * * * *

FOREWORD

To become a Buddhist is the easiest thing on earth. One does not have to sign any document to prove it, nor is one required to declare it before a witness. There is no ceremony to accept him, nor is there anybody to admit him into the fold of Buddhism. He simply becomes a Buddhist out of his own desire.

Lord Buddha is not God. He declared that he was not God and did not believe in the existence of one. Lord Buddha had no commandments to give. He only gave his advice. Whether anyone wanted to follow his advice or not was of little concern to him. It was one's own personal outlook. One can only save one's own self; Lord Buddha cannot save anybody. He has attained Nirvana and is out of this world, both in body and in spirit . . . a complete detachment.

Lord Buddha condensed his teaching for lay Buddhists to simple rules. There are only five rules for lay people, and whether one wants to follow them is a purely personal matter.

> Destruction of life is sinful.
>
> Stealing is sinful.
>
> Adultery is sinful.
>
> Telling a lie is sinful.
>
> Taking intoxicating drinks is sinful.

When a Buddhist becomes a Catholic, he is not asked to denounce all of these five rules. He is still forbidden to take human life, though he is entitled to defend himself and may be bound to defend others, even if this defense involves death for the aggressor. Wanton destruction of anything, living or inanimate, is still wrong for him. Stealing is sinful for a Catholic as for a Buddhist. So is adultery. So is falsehood. To take intoxicating drink to excess is sinful, as is eating to excess. Nor is one asked to denounce Lord Buddha. Buddha never claimed to be God. Certainly he meant well.

It is, indeed, not for us to judge God's plan. What God plans to do with a Buddhist or anyone else is entirely God's Will. On the other hand a seed, the word of God, knowingly or unknowingly sown by someone, may mean another step nearer to God. An act of charity shown may mean another step. Even a tear may speak with more eloquence than all the volumes of books ever written.

"Now no one, when he has lighted a lamp, covers it with a vessel, or puts it under a couch, but he puts it upon a lamp-stand, that they who enter may see the light."

(Luke VIII, 16)

BETTER THAN MONEY COULD BUY

I

"THE SEED FELL BY THE WAYSIDE"

> "The seed is the word of God. And those by the wayside are they who have heard; then the devil comes and takes away the word from their heart, that they may not believe and be saved."
>
> (Luke VIII, 11, 12)

During the first week after the opening of the school term, there was always great excitement among the boarders. Eagerly they told one another of the good times they had experienced during the long vacation. There were discussions on the new comers, new teachers, new roommates. Even the old big tree in the playground looked new.

All these things were important to the boys in the boarding school. It was real life and it was most interesting. To me, a boy of twelve years old, there were other things more important to occupy my mind. Such things as leaves on the playground, banana skins and paper which littered the ground were important. It meant work, the same kind of work that I had been doing in the school for the last two years. It was my duty to see that the compound of the school was always cleared of litter. Indeed I was

11

very proud of my work and for it I had the right to be paid half of my school fees. But this new term, other and more important things than banana skins and paper loomed up. Since I was already twelve years old, a bigger boy now, greater and more responsible duties were required of me in exchange for half the school fees. Besides keeping the school compound free of litter, I was also in charge of two classrooms which must be swept every day and washed once a week. Furthermore, after every meal I was to wash the dishes, too. These were the important things that occupied my mind during the first week of the re-opening of school.

Though wealth or poverty was no problem to me at that age, it was quite clear that there was a great difference between watching other boys eat ice-cream and eating it myself. I hardly have any recollection of my younger life, and what I knew then was very little indeed. I knew that I was an only child. My father, who was a medical officer in the Royal Thai Army, had been in jail since I was about three years old. He and his friends, mostly young army officers, thought that the absolute monarchical form of government was not good enough for the country. They wanted a real democracy, but the King did not quite agree with them. This resulted in my father and his friends being sentenced to life imprisonment.

I knew also that I had no home. My mother, who had managed to teach herself to read and write, was working as a temporary maid in various places. As a maid she had free meals and lodgings. She spent what she earned for the other half of my school fees. This much I knew.

I was doing quite well in my studies and was happy to be promoted to the third year of primary education. The school, a Protestant school, had

Biblical classes once a week. I often joined in these classes. The stories in the Old Testament were always interesting. The characters in the stories fascinated me. In the New Testament, Christ was my hero. Paul was also my hero. I attended enough Bible classes and had learned enough of the Gospel to be convinced that I wanted to be a Christian. So before I came back to school that term, I told my mother one evening all of what I knew about Jesus Christ. It took nearly an hour before I had finished . . .

She said, "Lert, from what you said about Jesus Christ, Mother thinks that He must be truly a great man. But why did you tell Mother about Him?"

"Mother," I replied, "I would like to be a Christian. Can I become a Christian?"

"Of course, you can," she said. "Following Christ's teaching, you would grow up to be a good man, and that is what Mother wants Lert to be."

Thus another important matter occupied my mind when I went back to school for the new term. The teacher had announced that those who had studied the Bible knowledge last year would be baptized soon—definitely before the end of the term. That was good news. I was delighted at the thought that very soon I would become a Christian. It would not be long now before I would be given the small square piece of bread in the Sunday communion service, the same as the boys in the front pews. I would eat it and put my head on the pew in front of me and say my prayers, too. Oh, how I wanted those pieces of square bread on the shining gold plate that was passed out to the people in the front pews! They never passed it to the back pews where I was told to sit. But this term I would have very little chance to join the Bible class, which was taught in the evening. There were too many banana skins and papers all over the compound. It took time to pick them all up. The classrooms were even worse. So many chairs had to be put over the desks and to be taken down again after the floor had been swept. By the time the two classrooms had been swept, it would be near meal time. But it could not be helped.

While I was kept busy with all these important things, there was talk about the school fees being raised. The matter of raising the school fee could not possibly have anything to do with me. The matter was furthest from my mind. I worked for my school fees and there was no reason why I should bother about their being raised. The other boys did not work for their school fees, so, of course, their parents would have to pay. This was good and sound logic to me.

At last the day was fixed for my Baptism. It was to take place in the church on a Sunday morning. All the boys who were to be baptized were told to put on their best clothes, complete with shoes and clean socks. I had no trouble about the best clothes, because the best ones I had were the only clothes I had. They were spotlessly clean, because I washed them myself with bits of soap that had been thrown away by other boys. But there was a bit of trouble with the socks. The only pair I had was not quite up to the mark, because one of the socks had been chewed to bits by a dog only the day before, while it was drying in the sun. But I could easily borrow a pair from a friend, and that was just what I did.

On this important Sunday I was ready. My clothes were clean, newly washed. I had a pair of borrowed socks and my shoes were really shining. We went to the church and sat down on the pews which had been allotted to us. Then came the auspicious moment. The boys to be baptized were told to get up and walk along the middle aisle, towards the altar, and I was among them. We stood in a long row in front of the rail. I was full of excitement and anticipation for the great ceremony.

While we were standing there, a teacher came up to check our names. When he came to my name, I noticed that something was wrong. The teacher took one look at me and, without saying a word, hurried away. Very soon he came back, pulled me out of the row and told me to get back to my seat. I shook his hand off and, looking at him, said, "Sir, I learned my Bible study all of last year and I want to be a Christian."

"Go back to your seat," was all he said to me.

I never saw the baptism ceremony. Although I put my head over the back of the pew in front of me, it was not to say my prayers, but to hide the tears that blinded my eyes. They would not give me the little square pieces of bread. They did not want me. They kept the bread for themselves only.

I was not to know the reason for my not being allowed to be baptized until a few weeks later. It was on a Saturday morning, while I was busy picking up the litter off the school compound, that I was called to the headmaster's room. I felt the tenseness of the atmosphere as soon as I entered the room, but the sight of my mother sitting on a chair overcame everything else. The headmaster was there, too, but I went straight to my mother, at the same time looking to see if she had brought any fruit with her. My eyes lit up when I saw a bunch of bananas on the floor beside her.

Mother caught hold of my hand in a very peculiar manner, one which I had never experienced before. She said: "Lert, you have to leave the school."

"I can't, Mother," I said. "The term is not over till another month."

"Mother came to pay for the school fees," she explained, "but Mother has not got enough money."

I could not understand about the school fees at all. Surely they knew that I worked for my school fees, at least for half of them, and if Mother came to pay for the school fees, surely she must have enough money, for she would never come otherwise. Perhaps it had something to do with the school fees being raised. So I asked her if that was the trouble. She nodded her head.

"Lert, my son," she said, "Mother walked all the way for nearly three miles to save the tram fares for this bunch of bananas for you. Mother has just received one whole month's wages, but it still is not enough for the school fees."

"Mother, not enough?" I still could not grasp the situation.

"The school fees," she explained, "were raised to twice as much as before and the headmaster says that you must pay full fees from now on."

"That's right, Lert," the headmaster, who had said nothing before, now added. "The school cannot afford to keep poor boys any longer."

"Sir," I tried to argue, "I have been working for my school fees. I even sweep the classrooms and wash the dishes now."

By this time the full realization that I must leave school had sunk into my head. The tears and the sobs must have wrenched Mother's heart. She pulled me nearer to her and I saw a new face looking up at me. It was my mother's face, but it seemed that I had never seen the likes of it before. She looked straight at me, and the way she looked stopped my tears. She said, "Lert, Mother and Lert are poor, but we are not beggars. We do not beg for charity. Charity is given and not begged. Come, Lert, do not waste any more tears. Tears are for love and not for want of money. Come, let us go, and Mother promises you that as long as Mother lives, Lert will have the best education that money can buy."

I went and collected my very few belongings. The whole school seemed to know all about my leaving. I was only a poor boy being ejected from school for not being able to pay his school fees. It was not even a sensation. Nobody wanted to ask any questions. They had heard it all from the school grape-vine. I had nobody to say goodbye to. It seemed a pity that I had not even finished picking up the litter. Now they would hire somebody else to do it, and I was sure it would cost them much less than half the school fees; otherwise they would have kept me.

While we were walking along the street after leaving the school compound, it struck me that I did not know where we were going. As far as I knew, we had no home. During the vacations, I was always sent to the home of one of our relatives, mostly out in the fishing village, or to relatives who owned rice farms in the country. When I questioned her, Mother said that she would ask my aunt who lived in town to keep me for the time being.

The afternoon sun was hot, and there seemed to be no end to that walk, but I was happy again. I was happy to see Mother and be with her, instead of merely visiting her as I customarily did every two or three months during the school year. Now I could be near her, talk to her and even help her in the house where she worked. I had often done this in the past and had been frequently rewarded with sweets. Mother had strictly forbidden me ever to take any money unless I had worked for it. I could not take any money for helping her because she was being paid for it already.

While walking and chatting with her, my mind went back to the sad event of a few Sundays ago. The raising of the school fees might have had something to do with my baptism. Yet I could not see how it could have happened. Perhaps the headmaster knew that I would be expelled from school soon. Or perhaps a poor boy cannot become a Christian. The problem was too much for me, and my mother certainly could explain it. She always explained everything, so I asked her.

We had just reached a big tree by the side of the road. It was cool in the shade of the tree. We both stopped, and I was glad for the rest. She was silent for a while, as if weighing something in her mind, before she answered my question.

"Lert," she said, "you told me that Christ was poor, that His mother and father were also poor. Mother does not understand why they did not baptize you."

"But it was true, Mother," I said. "They did not let me and did not tell me why."

She was silent again. She broke a banana off the bunch and handed it to me. Then she took one for herself and seemed to forget all about it, while I peeled mine and was glad to have it, for I was quite hungry by then. I had quite forgotten about the problem, when she said: "In the story you told me about Jesus Christ, somebody said something, I do not quite remember, but it was about — blessed are the hungry and those that thirst for justice, for they shall be satisfied. Lert, if you want justice, you must always be honest, and if you are honest, you will be satisfied. If you want to be a Christian and want to eat those little square pieces of bread, you have to be honest and sincere . . . then later on you will not be denied."

I had finished eating the banana, and Mother has just peeled hers and had thrown the skin down on the ground under the tree. Through habit I automatically bent down, picked up the banana skin and added it to my own in my hand. She looked at me and burst out laughing, but it took me a while before I saw what she was laughing at. Then I joined her. Mother and son laughed joyously under the cool shadow of the tree by the roadside.

Now, forty years after that hot Saturday afternoon, under the shade of the big tree, I understand what is meant in the book of St. Luke VIII, 11,12: "The seed is the word of God. And those by the wayside are they who have heard; then the devil comes and takes away the word from their heart."

II

"AND OTHER SEEDS FELL AMONG THORNS . . ."

"And that which fell among the thorns, these are they who have heard, and as they go their way, are choked by the cares and riches and pleasures of life."

(Luke VIII, 14)

For a whole year I moved from one place to another, from one aunt to another. I seemed to have a great number of aunts and uncles in town and could not quite remember with whom I had been staying. But it was very kind of all of them to keep me, even for a short time, for they were also poor relatives and an extra mouth to feed was an extra burden. Of course we had a few rich relatives, too, but Mother was adamant in her motto: Charity is given, not begged. None of it came our way, and none was begged for.

There was no hardship in my life as a vagabond boy; at least, I have no recollection of any. Life was full of fun, whether I lived with one aunt or another, whether I learned at this school or another or even in no school at all. Somehow, I seemed to get my education that year. I can count no less than four schools, during those twelve months, through which I briefly passed.

At last, another aunt took me in to stay with

her permanently. I was to work in the house, and my duties were clearly laid out for me on the first day of my arrival. I was to clean and polish the floors every morning and evening. I was to cook the rice, to go to the market and run errands. But the most important thing was that I would be sent to a good school. In return, I was to pay back whatever she had spent on me when I was big enough to earn my living. I nodded my head in acceptance of this arrangement, but Mother insisted on my repeating the promise, word for word, which I dutifully did.

Now Mother could come and see me any evening that she got off from work, and sometimes she could even spend the night with me. She did not have to worry about school fees any more. She saved most of her wages, and in a year she had enough money to buy a secondhand Singer sewing machine. When she was not employed, Mother was able to make simple skirts and blouses. Then she went from door to door to sell them.

Four years quickly slipped by, and one day Mother and my aunt came in bursting with excitement. The newspaper was full of news about a great celebration which was soon to take place. The occasion was the fifteenth anniversary of the King's coronation. On this day, the King was going to grant reprieve to many prisoners. Would the political prisoners be released, too, or perhaps their terms of imprisonment reduced? To me it did not matter, for as far as I was concerned, I never had a father. I had never known what it was like to have a father. That night I went to bed without giving the matter any more thought.

A few days later, excitement grew to a high pitch. The newspapers said that the political prisoners were to be released. The happiness, the laughs, the tears of joy were infectious, and I felt the excitement growing within me, without quite knowing the reason for it.

On the day the prisoners were to be released, Mother went out at 9 o'clock in the morning to wait at the prison gate. The prisoners were to be released at 10 o'clock. Lunch had been prepared before she went out. I stayed away from school that day and remained at home, waiting for my father. Time passed slowly; 10 o'clock came, then 11 o'clock. Still they had not come. My aunt began to worry, and my uncle was in a bad mood. By 12 o'clock there was no sign of my parents. By half-past twelve Mother came back alone, and questions were heaped upon her. What had happened? Why was he not released? When would he be released? Mother looked very tired. She said that it was very crowded at the prison gate, and everyone there also wanted the answers to these questions. The only information from the guard at the gate was that the prisoners were being released in groups from various sections all through the morning, and that the political prisoners would also be released. But he did not know who were to be released, nor when. That was all.

Mother took a bath, changed and we all started our lunch. None of us enjoyed that lunch. Conversation lagged. Mother was to go again at 2 p.m. to the prison. After lunch I went into the front room and took out a book to read. I had not read more than a page when Father walked in. I looked up and saw him standing there looking at me. His face looked grim without a trace of a smile. One word came out of my mouth. "Father!" I simply said.

He came over to me then, put his arm around my shoulder and quietly said, "Son." Together we went into the back room where the rest were sitting. The room was silent up to then; there was no conversation, and everyone was looking miserable and sad. We stopped and stood facing them. They looked up, stared at us without speaking. Time stood still. Then there was pandemonium.

Everybody was talking at once, and laughs mingled with their tears. When the excitement died down, Father explained that at 10 o'clock, he and his friends were taken out of the prison to the military headquarters and were officially informed of the King's proclamation of pardon. Then they were taken back to be presented to the superintendent of the prison, where the release orders were read. They signed their acknowledgment. Then at about 1 p.m. they were let out of the prison gate, and Father, finding nobody there to meet him, asked his way and came home as quickly as he could.

My aunt gave us a spare room, and for the first time in my life, Father, Mother and I were alone together. I slept soundly from sheer emotional exhaustion. It was a new experience to have a father. The kindness and love shown to me were unlike anything I had ever experienced. We often took long walks together in the evening, the three of us, and life was again full of happiness.

About two months later Mother said that we were to move into a new place, a home of our own. Father was to start his own medical clinic. One of my uncles in the country had lent him the money. Soon we found ourselves in our own home, which served as a clinic on the ground floor and living quarters on the second floor.

I found myself very much involved in this new kind of life. Father also opened a dispensary attached to the clinic, and I was put in charge of it. My duties were sweeping, cleaning, running errands, acting as sales boy and pharmacist under the supervision of my father. Father had asked me if I would forego my studies for two years in order to help him start this business, and had promised that after the two years he would send me to any school I wished. I was willing and happy to accept this arrangement, for I was proud of having been asked by my father and mother to help. Mother insisted that I be paid for my work with a reasonable wage. I was rich. In less than a year I had saved enough money to buy a bicycle, so that I did not have to walk any more. Soon after that I proudly possessed a camera and a complete set of photographic developing and printing equipment. Life was good to me.

Within two years Father had fully paid back the loan. He bought a house and a motor car. We could also boast of a speedboat. We were well-to-do indeed. Thus one day I was told that the time had come for me to start my schooling again.

I had by this time selected a Catholic missionary school—the best school in town, according to my information. Father and Mother had no objections but asked my reason for the choice. My reason was simple. I was convinced that this was where I could receive the best education that money could buy. Father remarked that he seemed to have heard this expression before, but Mother said nothing. Other thoughts seemed to be occupying her mind then.

So I was back to school again at the age of seventeen. School fees were no trouble this time, and there was no more picking up of litter and banana skins. By this time, too, Christianity had completely faded from my mind. There were other important things to preoccupy me; studies to catch up with, the work at home, friends to meet and my hobby, photography. Jesus Christ was furthest from my mind. Although this school occasionally reminded me of the former Protestant school, yet it was not the same. Here they said a lot of prayers, it seemed to me. Every day at the beginning and at the end of the class, prayers were said in English. After a while I noticed that the name of Mary was often mentioned in these prayers. It was mentioned in class, too, when the Brothers related stories of religious nature, but this made little impression on me.

During the next three years a strange curiosity about Mary began growing in me. Why did they call her "Holy Mary" and "Virgin Mary"? I knew that she was the Mother of Christ, but what had she done to be called holy? At the age of twenty I knew the meaning of the word virgin, but how could Mary be called a virgin if she were a mother? I found no answers to these questions.

One day, when all the students had gathered in the auditorium of the school to hear the results of the term's examination, one of my classmates who had been sitting next to me in class, was rewarded for being the best in catechism. I knew that there were catechism classes in the school and that many boys attended these classes. The word catechism confused me. I supposed it must have been some sort of Bible class.

That afternoon, after lunch, I was in no mood to join in any of the games which went on in the playground. I found myself standing on the wooden steps leading into the classroom. I was leaning against the wall gazing down at groups of boys playing and enjoying their games of marbles and football. Then I saw my friend who had been given the reward only that morning for being the best in catechism. His name was Somboon and he was walking towards me. In his hand was a small paper bag of peanuts, which he was munching. He came over to the steps and stopped beside me. He handed

the bag of peanuts to me saying: "Take some nuts.
They are not crispy anyway."

I took a few and, munching them, I added:
"Somboon, what was the reward you got this
morning?"

"A book," he answered, and continued eating
the nuts.

"What book?" I asked.

"A book about a saint," he replied, and gazing
around said, "How about a game of marbles?"

"I don't want to play today," I answered.

"Why?" he asked. I answered that I was busy.

"Busy doing nothing? Come on. If you have
no marbles, I can lend you one. Here, come."

"Really, I don't want to play," I said again.
"I am busy — busy thinking."

"Oh, the professor is busy thinking," Somboon
said, "and may I ask what he is thinking about?"

I did not seem to be doing very well in my
questioning, for all these questions were not the ones
that I wanted to ask at all. It was difficult to be
point blank, but I tried again.

"Somboon," I said, "what do you learn in your
catechism class?"

"Is that really what you are thinking about?"
he asked. I nodded.

"Well, we learn the Gospel, you know, the
story of Jesus Christ and His teachings. We learn
about liturgy, sacraments and lots of other things.
Now will you play marbles with me?"

He was all for a game of marbles. He wanted
to try to win back what he had lost to me the other
day.

"What is liturgy?" I asked.

"It's about Holy Mass and other ceremonies," he replied.

The thing was getting worse and worse. I got nowhere near what I wanted to know. The more I asked, the more I got confused, but I doggedly persisted and asked again.

"What is Holy Mass?"

"The Holy Mass," he began to answer, then broke off, saying: "Lert, I have had enough catechism in class already, and will you stop bothering me by asking these sort of questions?" He began to walk away.

I was desperate. If I let him go now, I would never have enough courage to ask him or anyone else again. So I caught hold of his arm to stop him and said hurriedly:

"Somboon, why do you call Mary holy?"

"Mary is holy," he replied, "because she was the Mother of God."

"But the other Christians do not call her holy," I said.

"What other Christians? Do you mean the Protestants?" he asked. I nodded my head.

"Well, I'm not a Protestant," he added. "I'm a Catholic."

"Oh, I see." But I really did not see at all.

I hurried on again and asked, "What about Virgin Mary?"

"Virgin Mary?" he said. "What about her?"

"Is she a virgin?" I asked.

"Of course, she is a virgin, and holy, too," he replied.

"But how could she be a virgin?" I argued. "She had a husband and a son."

"Of course, she is virgin," he persisted. "It is

in the Gospel, and I can show it to you. She was never with Joseph, and the Gospel said so."

"It cannot be," I said. "If she was not with Joseph, then she was not faithful to Joseph. She must have been with other men."

I did not realize the effect of my argument until I saw his face. He had actually turned white and both hands clenched into fists. The bag of peanuts burst and the nuts spilled to the ground. I was not afraid of him, because I knew that I could beat him any time, even though he was slightly bigger than I. But he made no attempt to raise his hands against me. Instead, I noticed tears starting to run down his face. He shook his head as if to rid himself of something. Abruptly he turned and walked away, without even bothering to wipe the tears from his face.

I was left alone again. I felt no sympathy or sorrow for what I had done. He had no cause to cry, and I thought him to be very uncooperative. I was disappointed with the whole thing.

The next morning, after the usual prayers, I turned to him and said, "Somboon, why did you cry yesterday?"

He did not answer, so I tried again. "I don't know anything about Mary. That is why I asked," I said.

"You insulted the Mother of God," he replied.

"No, I did not. I only asked you," I said.

"You certainly did!" he insisted.

"I did not!" Before I could say any more there was a summons from the Brother:

"Lert and Somboon, come here!"

The whole class was in complete silence. Both of us got up and walked over to the Brother.

"Both of you were talking in class. Who started it?" he asked.

Both of us replied in unison. "I did, Brother."

We looked at one another in surprise and before we could explain any more, the Brother smiled and said: "So, both of you started it. Very well, both of you on your knees in front of the class."

We knelt down on the floor, side by side in front of the class and turned to one another with a smile on our faces. The smile was more eloquent than any words. It explained everything. We were friends again.

Though the hunger and the thirst for truth still remained, the whole episode was pushed to the back of my mind. I had many other important things to do—my studies, my work at the dispensary, meeting my friends, and photography. We had a house, owned a piece of land, had a motor car, a speedboat, and I had a bicycle and a camera. I was preoccupied with these things.

But the seed was planted, and unknowingly I had taken my first step towards Christianity.

Thus it is written in the Gospel of St. Luke VIII, 14: "And that which fell among the thorns, these are they who have heard, and as they go their way are choked by the cares and riches and pleasures of life. . . ."

III.

"AND OTHER SEED FELL UPON THE ROCK . . . "

> "Now those upon the rock are they who, when they have heard, received the word with joy; and these have no root, but believe for a while, and in time of temptation fall away."
>
> (Luke VIII, 13).

Before I could reach the university, I needed two years more in the secondary school and I was already twenty-one years old. The realization that age was running ahead of me only stirred me to greater ambition. Thus one evening, I carefully dropped a "bomb" by saying: "Father, I am going to be a doctor."

I waited to see the effect of my bold announcement.

"You mean that you want to be a doctor, Lert," he said.

"No, Father," I replied. "I am going to be a doctor. 'Wanting to be' is only a wish, and 'going to be' is a determination and conviction."

"I doubt if you will succeed," he said, "because so far you have shown neither the ability nor the stamina required for such a difficult course of study. In any case, you still have two more years of study to think it over."

"I have told you my decision, Father," I went on, "and it is time that I must tell you, because I would like to go to the Hong Kong University for medical studies. In order to enter the Hong Kong University, I should go to pre-university school in Hong Kong for at least two years, before I can take the matriculation examination. Will you permit me?"

I looked at my mother, hoping for strong support from her. She would not meet my eyes but kept her eyes on Father and said: "I don't want him to go to Hong Kong. It's too far away from home."

This was really a bad start, but I had determined to argue my way through, so I went on:

"Mother, I know that you have always trusted me, so your objection must be due to a fear of danger. I am not afraid. I can take care of myself now."

"Lert, we have always been together through years of hardship and poverty. Now when we are so happy together . . ." She did not finish the sentence. The lump in her throat was hard to swallow.

"Yes, Mother," I agreed. "But you have Father now, and I want the best education that money can buy."

It was cruel and I knew it, yet I must not give in under any circumstances.

"Lert, Mother knows, and Mother is glad to have said that, so many years ago. But Hong Kong is so far away, so very far away."

"Lert, it requires money to buy an education, and we don't have that kind of money," Father interrupted.

I smiled to myself inwardly. Everything was going according to my plan. Sentimentality was pushed aside, and hard cash was brought into the picture. I pounced on the advantage that was unwittingly offered.

"It costs no more than 120 pounds sterling per year, Father. Only ten pounds sterling a month."

"That is nonsense," Father said unbelievingly. "Have you investigated?"

"I don't doubt him at all," Mother said. "He always plans things a long time ahead, so that he has all the details at his finger tips. He planned this discussion, too."

Father ignored the comment, for he still had one more card up his sleeve, and he used it.

"No doubt we can afford ten pounds a month, but we cannot afford 120 pounds, plus the fare to Hong Kong," he objected.

I knew that this was his last card and a very weak one. As Mother had said, I had planned this discussion and had expected such an argument, so I had my answer ready. I wanted the permission pronounced there and then, so I said: "I have saved up some money for the passage. It isn't quite enough yet, but I still have a few months to go. I don't need 120 sterling to carry with me. Only half of that will do."

Mother saw that Father had lost his fight by falling into my well-planned trap. But she would not give in.

"Lert, you cannot go," she said. When she spoke these words, I knew that I was going to have a very difficult time. It would be the final parry and it was going to be something I had not counted on. She then dropped her "bomb."

"Lert, as a Buddhist, your duty as an only son is to join the priesthood. You are now of age. Your duty to your Mother and Father must come before your education." This was a bigger "bomb" than the one that I had dropped.

She was right. As an only son and a Buddhist, my foremost duty was towards my parents. A Thai is a Buddhist from birth. He learns about Buddhism from his mother's knee, even before he is able to speak. He is taught to perform the *wai,* a gesture of respect used by the Thai, by putting both hands with palms together and lifting them up towards the face, while at the same time bowing the head. (It is used primarily as an act of reverence upon meeting a monk.) He lives and grows in the atmosphere of Buddhist culture from birth to death. Throughout his entire life, his activities revolve around the Buddhist temple — from the naming of the child, the treating of aches and pains, or building a house to cremating of the dead. His behavior in front of a monk is always one of great reverence. He is most careful in his words and deeds, in fear of tempting the monk towards worldly desire. For such a sin he would be despised and abhorred by all.

Such is the Buddhist life into which I was born. I grew up in its fold and was molded into its cast without any formal instruction, but rather by simply living it. One becomes a Buddhist by living the Buddhist life, not by any overt act of admission. There is no formal admission into Buddhism, nor is one required to make a declaration of his intention, even if he was not a Buddhist before but desires to become one. It is indeed the easiest thing on earth to become a Buddhist. One is born into it or simply becomes one by living it. It is easier still to live as a Buddhist, for nobody will ask you to denounce anything. There is no such being in Buddhism as

God, and to believe in such would be regarded as unnecessary if not unwarranted.

Thus as a Buddhist, I had only five simple rules to follow, rules taught by the Lord Buddha. These were briefly:

Destruction of life is sinful,

Stealing is sinful,

Adultery is sinful,

Telling lies is sinful,

Taking intoxicating drinks is sinful.

These are not commandments, but rather guiding rules for a lay Buddhist. Lord Buddha declared more than 2,500 years ago to his disciples that he was not a god. Therefore he could neither command nor save anybody. He preached: "One can only save oneself." If his words did not lead one to see the light of truth, then he could do no more to help.

I was not, therefore, bound legally by any commandments. If by my words or by my deeds a life were destroyed, be it that of a plant, animal or man, I would be held responsible for it. The outcome of my present life and the state of my spirit after death depended entirely upon such actions on my part. No sin was forgivable, for sin was something which one committed against one's own self, not against anybody else. The deed done demanded retribution to be made either in this life or in a life after death, or in both. When and in what form this retribution would take place, nobody knows. The performance of a good deed did nothing towards minimizing the consequence of sin, but it did have some sort of nebulous merit applicable to me or my parents either in this life or in the life after death.

Although there was no monk to see that I live according to the Lord Buddha's teaching, there was one great ruler and punisher in the person of my mother, who made sure that I broke none of the five rules. A violation of these rules would bring the maternal wrath upon my head. Indeed, this was a most effective persuasion against sin, as far as a Buddhist of my standing was concerned. I realized with painful experience that the repetition of such wrongdoing would result in nothing but woe for myself.

No doubt, having grown up beyond the length of the stick in my mother's hand, I was free, but the teaching, training and the stick had done their job well. The formation during my childhood in the sphere of Buddhism had been successfully completed. The rest was up to me. Thus it was left to me to fulfill my duty towards my parents by joining the Buddhist priesthood for three months.

I had learned a certain amount of Buddhism in various Buddhist schools, and Mother and I had talked often about the teachings of the Lord Buddha, so that she knew what I thought about becoming a Buddhist monk. She respected my opinion, and the question of my entering the priesthood for the traditional three months had never been mentioned before. Both of us had agreed that if Lord Buddha himself could not offer anybody spiritual grace, it was obvious that a person entering priesthood could not possibly obtain such grace for anyone but himself, if this sort of grace existed.

I regretted my having used my cherished expression "to have the best education money can buy," as a lever to force my father into consenting to my trip. If I spared no punches, Mother was not going to spare any either. It was fair enough. I hated to leave her but I must go. I must not lose my head now. Somehow, I sensed that Father realized the fight was still on, but that my hesitation showed that I was losing ground. He was out of the arena now and took no part. My daring had served its purpose. I wondered if I should try again by challenging my mother directly on a point of belief. Did she really believe that my becoming a monk would result in spiritual grace for her? However, it was clear that she had adopted my method of argument and that very likely such a point of attack would lead me into another trap. I thought hard and decided to abandon this tack. There was only one course left, and I turned to it.

"Do I have your permission then to go to Hong Kong if I enter the Buddhist priesthood?" I asked.

At all costs, I must get this permission and leave the rest for the future. She was disappointed, for it was not the answer that she had expected. I had eluded her. I had gained the lead again, and she could do nothing else but follow. She said: "Yes, I will let you go after you have fulfilled the traditional three months of priesthood."

Seeing that Mother had lost the fight, Father chuckled and said: "Lert, I don't need any of the spiritual graces from your becoming a Buddhist priest. You can give it all to Mother."

The thought struck me that if Father could stay fourteen years in jail, I could spend three months in the monastery, and be able to cherish the hope that I would then be able to go to Hong Kong.

"In any case," Mother said, pursuing the subject, "you cannot enter priesthood this year, because there are only eight days left before the beginning of the Buddhist Lent."

It was understood, of course, that one should enter the priesthood at the proper time, and this was the beginning of the Buddhist Lent. It lasted three months. I was not at all happy about this. The delay of three months and one year was unthinkable.

"It is not too late, Mother," I said.

"Lert, it's impossible," Mother answered. "It takes at least six months for anyone to prepare to enter into the priesthood. You know that very well."

"Mother," I said, "I know all about it. There are about 20 to 30 pages of prayers, questions and answers that I must know by heart for the ceremony. Besides, there will be two monks as sponsors by my side in case I go wrong somewhere. I could easily learn the 30 pages in three days and you can check on me."

"No abbot would consent to admit you in such a short time," she persisted.

"Then," I said, "let us go and see him tomorrow. No — let us go and see him today . . . now!"

Mother looked at Father. He smiled again and told Mother: "Count me out of this. The spiritual benefit is all yours."

All my relatives were told of the glad news, and Father and Mother were showered with congratulations. For me there was nothing but sympathy and understanding from my friends. Doubts were also expressed about my ability to last the required three months' period. Bets were even made among friends that I would not last more than three weeks, for a monk is only allowed two meals a day. The morning meal is taken at about 8 o'clock in the morning and the last meal shortly before noon. From noon until sunrise the next day I would not be permitted to partake of any food, except water or plain tea. The daily fast from noon onwards till sunrise the next day necessitated the consumption of a heavy meal in the morning, so that by 11:30 a.m.

it was impossible to eat much more. This, in turn, gave rise to an overwhelming hunger in the evening. I had a few doubts myself as to whether I would be able to endure the fast for three months.

I was greatly surprised when I was told by the abbot that I was required to know more than just the 20 or 30 pages necessary for the ordination ceremony. To be a monk, I must also know the rules and regulations laid down by the Lord Buddha for monks. There were more than 200 of these rules and they had to be observed to the letter. An infringement of any one of these rules must be confessed to another monk, and a more serious one could result in expulsion from the priesthood. The abbot was good enough to accept me into the monkhood on condition, however, that I would conscientiously study these rules during the three-month period, together with the Lord Buddha's teachings and their interpretations.

Early in the morning of the day of the ordination, my head and eyebrows were shaved. I changed from ordinary clothes into a white robe and cloak. For hours I had to sit and listen to the story of my conception; my life in Mother's womb was described in detail. The burden of suffering my mother had to go through at my birth was thoroughly dwelt on. The worries and cares of bringing me up were stressed. How grateful I should be to her for all this, and even for the milk with which she nourished me. In conclusion, it was pointed out that my becoming a monk was the most important duty towards my parents. The spiritual grace derived from this good deed would, I was assured, lead them to heaven. I sincerely hoped so, too.

At 11:30 a.m. I had my lunch. I ate as much as I could, for I would not get another meal till 8 the next morning. The two monks who had sponsored me then led me in procession three times around the assembly hall, followed closely by my father carrying the bowl which I would need to collect my food every morning. My mother was carrying the saffron robe, and my friends carried the other necessary items which would be offered to me for use during my priesthood. Everybody was happy, but the sun was strong and hot, and I was tired and beginning to get hungry again, though it was not quite two hours since my lunch.

Inside the assembly hall, along one side, sat a row of nine monks. In front of me stood tier upon tier of gold and bronze Buddha images, before which sat the abbot who was the minister for the ceremony. We all sat down facing the abbot, myself in front with the other people behind.

Presenting myself before the abbot, I began by giving him the usual salutation. Then chanting in a loud voice, I begged to be admitted into the order of the priesthood. Questions were asked: Was I in normal health? Was I physically fit? Was I willing to denounce the world and its affairs? Did I owe anyone anything? Had anybody any moral claim on my person? If anyone had, let that person declare his claim! These questions were asked three times to make absolutely sure that I was a free man and that nobody in the world had any claim on me whatsoever. Nobody raised a claim, and the ceremony moved on.

My white garment was then taken off, and I was cloaked in the saffron robe. The food bowl was hung on my back and I went again to the abbot. The monks who sponsored me declared that I was eligible for the priesthood in accordance with the rules set up by the Lord Buddha. The ritualistic prayers were recited, more advice given, and I was a monk.

I had announced the news of my becoming a monk to the boys at school the day before my ordination. It was a great joke and a sensation. The Brother hearing the news thought it was a great joke, too. He laughed heartily and reminded me that I must not forget about my homework for the next day. I told him that I would send my homework through a classmate, but that I would be absent from school for a day, on account of the ordination ceremony.

The next day after my ordination, I went to school as usual and sat in my ordinary place, but now dressed as a Buddhist monk. This was even a bigger sensation. It was unheard of that a Buddhist priest should sit learning in a Catholic school. It was practically an affront to the Brothers, and poor Brother professor was most unhappy. He consulted with his Superior and asked me to see him. During recess, I went to see him and was told that I should not have come to school under such conditions. He wanted to know why I did not stay where I belonged, in the monastery.

I hold him that I saw no reason why a monk should not go to school and that I did not think that I had broken any rules or regulations of the school by coming in saffron robes. He pleaded with me and pointed out that I was the cause of disturbance in the class just by sitting there with my shaven head, shaven eyebrows, saffron robes and sandals. It was too much for the students. I saw his point and agreed to resign from the school. In turn, I was given an excellent recommendation from Brother Director.

My life as a Buddhist monk was one long

continuous monotony. I was cut off from the outside world which I had willingly and voluntarily renounced. I had no claim whatsoever on the world, and the world had no claim on me. When I shed the last piece of lay garment just before being cloaked in the saffron robes, I had shed my last possession on earth. Even the saffron robes were simple yellow-colored pieces of material which had been kindly offered by people for the purpose of covering my body. I had no claim on them for they did not belong to me.

No monk can presume ownership over anything worldly, for he is no longer of this world. For instance, if a layman accidentally touches the robe of the monk in passing on a street, immediately upon reaching his cell in the monastery, the monk must shed that robe. He has no right to wear it any more. It is agreed that the touch on the robes by a layman is sufficient to dispute the monk's right to use them. The same principle applies to what a monk himself may or may not touch. Since the monk has no claim on the world, he may touch nothing which belongs to somebody else, unless it is clearly offered to him. And this must be done on the part of the layman by holding out both hands in an explicit gesture of offering, or, in the case of a large object or immovable thing, by stating in no uncertain terms that this is an offering pure and simple..

Life was peaceful, but meaningless and useless. If Lord Buddha was right in saying that "one can only save oneself," then I could not possibly help anybody else spiritually anyway. But I had committed myself and I intended to carry out the commitment in the best way I could. If it was not going to benefit anybody else except myself, then I was going to make sure of obtaining that benefit to the full. I, therefore, made up my mind that during the three months' period I would concentrate on learning as much as possible about Buddhism. The National Library was full of Lord Buddha's teachings and interpretations, and I conscientiously made full use of it.

I dutifully got up every morning at 5:30 a.m., dressed myself with meticulous care according to the rules, and went out to receive the food offered by the people of the district. The people would be waiting outside their front gates with cooked rice, fish, meat, sweets and fruits ready to put some of this into the bowl which I carried. I said a thanks-giving prayer in silence for each one of them.

It must be understood, however, that a Buddhist monk does not beg. But since he is completely detached from this world, he has not even a kitchen for cooking. He lives by what people offer to him. Such an offering is an act of virtue which brings spiritual merit to the one offering. It is the monk's obligation not to deprive the people of such merit, and therefore, unless the monk is bed-ridden with sickness, he must go out to receive these offerings each morning.

I would walk past the houses and if I were shown a sign of invitation, I would stop and receive the offering. This was obligatory on my part. Even if my bowl happened to be full, I could not refuse. It would be a sin for me to deprive a person of this merit. The rice, fish, meat, sweets and fruit in the bowl would be pressed down by the good people so that more could be added.

I had to be back at the monastery before 8 a.m. The food and the rice were sorted out by the service boy, and I could sit down to my well-earned meal. For a Buddhist monk, food is taken solely for the

preservation of life. To derive wilful pleasure from
it would be a sin. Furthermore, it would be a sin
to deprive the people who offered the food of their
merit by not eating it. I must therefore eat one
mouthful of each kind of food in turn. To pick and
choose any particular kind was a sin. When the
meal was finished, more thanksgiving prayers were
offered for my kind donors.

After breakfast I settled down to a serious study
of the monk's rules and the Lord Buddha's teachings.
At 11 a.m. the drum in the tower would announce
that the second and last meal for the day could be
taken. The remainder of the food from the morning
would be brought over. I had to finish my meal
before noon. After that, no food in any form could
pass my lips.

Before going to bed the last thing to do was
to make my daily confession. I might have accidentally stepped on some unseen insect, hurt it or
even killed it. Perhaps, I had wanted to look with
admiration at the woman who was giving the offering
this morning or I had enjoyed bathing in the cool
pond next to the monastery. These were sins. I
had to confess all of them. To me this confession
was an empty ritual, for I could not bring myself
to feel sorry for some of these so-called sins. When
the mosquitoes were fierce, I swatted them, consoling
myself by the thought that they had now paid with
their lives for their sins of a previous life and hoped
that they might now reach heaven.

One day, I declared that it was time I completed
my act of merit-making by giving my parents the
ordination sermon. I consulted my sponsor monks,
but they refused to have anything to do with it. I
then consulted the abbot and he laughed. "My dear
Reverend," he said, "I know that you have talent,

but to appear in public and to give a sermon is not possible now. Perhaps in another two or three years."

Obedience was one of the rules. The next week I went again to see him. I had asked for 45 minutes of privacy with him. During that time I recited to him the whole ritual required, including the sermon to be given. After my exhibition he said: "Dear Reverend, you have not disappointed me. I am not ignorant of your diligence, but objections have been raised against such an early undertaking. However, I am satisfied. You have my permission."

I send word to my parents that they should now request my sermon, for I could not preach without being requested.

To be doubly sure of not making any mistakes or of forgetting any part, I inscribed most of the necessary parts that I would have to recite on the palm-leaf fan, which I would have to hold in front of my face while I was chanting. Thus with full confidence I preached to my parents.

Calmly I sat on the daïs prepared for me and started, as required by the rule, by asking if the congregation were willing and ready to hear words of the Lord Buddha. When the congregation gave their approval, I asked them if they wanted to accept and carry out the five rules for laymen directed by the Lord Buddha. Those who were willing to accept, repeated these rules after me. Those who did not want to accept any given rule could simply ignore whatever rule they did not care to keep.

The sermon was no trouble, for I had learned it all by heart, and the chanting was perfect. But somehow the atmosphere was not right. I felt that Mother was there purely because it was unavoidable. There was no monetary offering, as I had hopefully expected. She was not interested. She simply said, "Your Reverence, you are very talented and I have much admiration for you. My offerings to you are flowers, candles and incense. This is all you need as a monk to offer to Lord Buddha, that I might derive merit from the sermon."

That night I added another item to my confession. I had been sinful in desiring wealth and in being discontented over not receiving it.

These few weeks in the life of the Buddhist priesthood convinced me that I would never attain Nirvana.[1] No matter what I did, it was sinful. It would have been better for me to remain as a layman, for then I would not have committed so many sins. The longer I stayed in the priesthood, the more sins I was piling up, and none of them were forgivable. Even as a layman, with only five rules to hold, I realized that I could not keep account of the number of lives that I destroyed every day. Each day I added an untold amount of punishment for myself and for my spirit after death.

There was no salvation for me, and with this loss of hope, I lost faith in Buddhism. I could never get anywhere near the eternal peace of Nirvana, no matter how I tried. Life was no better than a candle to be consumed by the flame. When the wax was totally consumed, there was no more candle, no more life. It was the end.

The seed, the word of God, which I had heard with joy years ago, fell upon the rock, for it had no root and in time of temptation, died. The ambition to become a doctor had lured me into the Buddhist monkhood. Now I must pursue this ambition once again and set my thoughts on the promised trip to Hong Kong.

IV.

"AND OTHER SEED FELL UPON GOOD GROUND."

> "But that which fell upon good ground, these are they who, with a right and good heart, having heard the word, hold it fast."
>
> (Luke VIII, 15).

The time passed quickly and the three months' period was over. In two weeks I was in Hong Kong. A friend who had been one of my schoolmates met me at the ship and took me over to the new school to meet the Director. I had no trouble in being admitted.

The fact that I again found myself in a Catholic school did not matter to me. Religion of any kind meant nothing to me at all. If my father was an atheist, I was, by comparison, a total skeptic. My concentrated study of Buddhism, though greatly adding to my knowledge of the subject, only helped to drive me further away. If it is true, according to Lord Buddha's doctrine, that desire is the root of all obstacles which prevent one from attaining Nirvana, then I had no hope whatsoever of obtaining Nirvana. Eternal peace is certainly the ultimate aim of anyone. And if Nirvana is a state of eternal peace, then I certainly wanted it. But even this desire, the desire to attain it, to aim for it, to live for it and to act for it, automatically prevents one from attaining it. I would have lost the battle before I had even begun.

The Irish Jesuits who owned and ran the school were a new experience to me. They were kind and understanding, but, it seemed to me, unreasonably strict. Yet I had to admit that this strictness was tempered with fairness and friendliness, and I could not help but love them. No direct approach to convert me was ever made. I was distrustful all the same and on my guard. Even things like invitations to exchange stamps, for instance, struck me as suspicious, and I purposely ignored them. I wanted a doctor's degree, not another form of religion.

I studied hard, but my English was poor and the London matriculation examination papers were not easy. I often studied late into the night, although according to the school regulations lights were to be out by 10 p.m.

One night I was kept very late, trying to solve an algebra problem, and I was sleepy. The only way to get it over and finished with, was to go and see Father Dan, my class master. It was around 11 p.m. and everything was dark, but as I approached Father Dan's room, I saw that the light in his room was still on, so I knocked and went in. Piles of exercise books were beside him and he was busy correcting our homework. He looked up and said: "What? Not in bed yet?"

"No, Father," I replied. "I have spent over an hour on this and still cannot get it right."

He looked annoyed but asked me to show him my work. I showed it to him. He looked at it for a moment and then handed it back to me, saying:

"You applied the wrong formula. This is the one you should have used." Then he gave me the correct formula.

I was grateful to him and, picking up my book, was about to leave when he said: "Sit down, Lert. I am glad you came. All this homework — your homework — makes me feel tired."

I sat down, embarrassed, for I had no comment to make. After a moment, I said: "I am tired, too, and the matriculation examination is so near. My mathematics are all right, but my English is poor. I will never make it."

"Well, you never know," said Father Dan. "What is your aim for a career?"

"I want to be a doctor, Father." I replied.

"The healer of the body, a doctor," he commented. "Now that's interesting. And why do you want to be a doctor?"

"My father is a doctor."

"Now, Lert, I asked you why do you want to be a doctor," he said. "I did not ask you why other people become doctors."

"Well," I said, "I want to help the suffering."

"And why do you want to help the suffering?" he asked.

This was too much for me. I was tired and sleepy and wanted to go to bed, but I could see that Father was wide-awake and had completely forgotten about the homework. Before I realized it, I shot back at him, saying, "And why did you come all the way from Ireland to teach me mathematics and science?"

"Well now, Lert," he said, "for the life of me, I wouldn't have come here to teach you mathematics and science at all. It's my Superior, God help him,

who made me do it. I came here, and I'm telling
you the truth, to bring souls back to God. So, God
help me, for two years I've done nothing of the
kind."

That outpouring not only confounded me, but
his sincerity and feeling enkindled something in my
heart and soul. Covering up my confusion, I asked
him a question which must have been in my subconscious mind for some time. I said, out of the
blue:

"Father, you are a scientist, are you not? A
doctor of science?"

"That I am," he said. "And I can tell you,
it took quite some time to get that degree."

"Now, Father," I continued, "how can you, a
scientist, believe in such a thing as the Bible, which
was written by dreamers, and especially the New
Testament, written by uneducated fishermen?"

"Now you are talking, Lert," he said. "Sure,
I believe in the Bible — every word of it — God
knows. Sure, those people who wrote it were
ignorant of trigonometry and organic and inorganic
chemistry, but they were not ignorant of Jesus Christ.
Besides, they had the Holy Ghost with them, otherwise they would have been no better than you or I,
if not worse."

"Well, Father," I said, "I still don't know how
you can believe them. I can't."

"I know how you feel, Lert," he said. "You
can't say that I am more stupid than you are, and
no stupid fool can be given a degree of doctor of
science. But there is a simpler way to explain it.
Now the Bible was written, as you say, by dreamers,
uneducated dreamers, and yet hundreds of millions
of people like me, and not stupid people, you must
admit, believe in it now, and have believed, for

thousands of years. Now you — and you are not stupid but intelligent and educated — why don't you write something like that, and see who will believe it? I for one will not believe it, and if I do, God help me, I will be the one who is stupid, and not you."

I knew that he had me in a corner and I could extricate myself only by beating a hasty retreat. I rose abruptly, saying, "Good-night, Father," and left.

My defeat, my rashness in trying to pit my logic against a Jesuit, more than convinced me that I was no match for Father Dan. I consoled myself with the thought that at any rate a defeat in logic means neither that one is convinced of a truth nor making a voluntary admission of belief.

"All right," I said to myself. "You win the first round, Father Dan, but there will be a second round to come."

The second round came unexpectedly and caught me just as unprepared as the first round. Again it was mathematics — a geometry problem, which had kept me up to midnight, and was still unsolved. As a last resort, I went to Father Dan's room again and found the light still burning. He did not look up, when I entered, until he had finished correcting the last few exercise books. I stood and waited, and when he finished, he stood up and said: "Go to bed. It is late, and you've broken the school regulations again. All lights out at ten o'clock!"

"Father, I cannot do this one, and the examinations are only a few days away," I pleaded.

"It will be explained in class tomorrow," he said. "Ah, well, sit down anyhow."

I sat down and opened my book to show him the problem, but he took one look and pushed the book back to me, saying: "Lert, your mathematics are all right. Don't worry over them. The matric paper never gets anywhere near what you are doing now, anyhow."

"I know, Father," I said. "I have been working on a few of the exam papers, but I should be able to solve this problem. I spent almost two hours at it and I still can't do it."

"I understand," he said. "But have you always succeeded in solving all the problems in your life?"

"No, Father," I admitted, "not all of them."

"Well, Lert," he said, "I couldn't, either. For instance, I became a priest to serve God. I volunteered to be a missionary to come to China, because I thought that millions and millions of souls were waiting for me to bring them back to God. I was overjoyed when I was sent here, but for three years — what have I done? I did not convert a single soul. Instead, I have corrected thousands and thousands of exercise books. God help me, but I sure don't know why."

I thought of a few reasons, but none of them seemed to be convincing and I had to reject them all. Observing my silence, he opened a drawer in his desk and took out a piece of toffee, looked at it reflectively and gave it to me saying: "Have a toffee. It's past midnight, and I can't eat it anyway."

I unwrapped the toffee, put it in my mouth and mumbled my thanks to him. He looked at me and asked: "What are the problems you could not solve?"

Something in my mind seemed to snap and, without thinking, the words popped out of my mouth — only two words: "Virgin Mary!"

I stared at him and was greatly surprised at myself. I saw his hand move towards the drawer again, open it and take out another toffee. He looked at it longingly, but dropped it into the drawer and slowly pushed the drawer back to place.

"And what did the Virgin Mary do to you?" he asked.

"She didn't do anything to me, Father, but why do you call her virgin? I can't understand."

"So that's what's troubling you then," he remarked. "Well now, Lert, this is not as difficult as that geometry problem. We can solve it in a much shorter time than those silly old straight lines, angles and triangles and circles, that is, if you are willing to hear, try to understand and not simply argue for the sake of arguing."

"Father, it's much too late to argue, and the other night about the Bible, I was not arguing. I asked because I wanted to know."

It was out now. I did not plan it and never even thought of it. The Virgin Mary had been forgotten a long time ago, but the question was back again now.

"You are right, Lert, it's much too late even for the problem of why Mary is a virgin. But since you are willing to solve it now, and I am willing to help you, let's go on our knees and say a short prayer before we begin."

He got up from his chair and automatically I got up, too, and said.

"Father, I do not say any prayers."

"What in the world is wrong with you?" he practically shouted at me. "A prayer won't kill you, and how can we learn the word of God without the help of the Holy Ghost anyhow?" Then he was down on his knees, made the sign of the cross and started: "Come, Holy Ghost..."

I was down on my knees, too. I had no prayer to say, and even if I had, I did not know to whom I would say it. I could only think, "I don't know who the Holy Ghost is, but if there is one and He can help me to understand about the Virgin Mary, well, I don't know, but —"

By this time Father Dan had finished his prayer and was up again. I also got up and then both of us sat down.

"Well, Lert," he began, "you know about the conception of human beings, don't you?"

"Yes, Father," I said. "I know about that. The male principle fusing with the female."

"Right you are," he said. "I expected you knew about it already, your father being a doctor and all that." Then he continued:

"So the male element must fuse with the female, and that is the conception of a human being. Next question is, where does the first male element come from, in order to fuse with the first female? You can't answer that, of course, and if you can, you are better than I, because I can't answer it, either."

"But, Father," I said, "this Adam business has nothing to do do with the virginity of Mary."

"Ah, now," he said, "but it has. We have to begin somewhere, don't we? This is as good a beginning of our problem as anything else. Surely you don't think that your ancestors were monkeys as Julian Huxley said, do you? And even if Julian Huxley's great-great-grandfather was a monkey, as he thought, then where did the first monkey come from anyway? To go back still further, if the first monkey came from a single-cell jellyfish, which is the same as saying that man comes from a jellyfish, then tell me...where does the first jellyfish come from? And I'll deny till doomsday that it came from the sand or the seaweed at the bottom of the sea, Huxley or no Huxley."

Since I had no comment to make to that, he went on: "So now we are back to poor Adam again, whether we like it or not. Anyhow, if you don't like the word 'Adam,' let's call the first man 'A,' which will suit our purpose just as well."

He stopped, but still I had no comment to make, and he continued:

"And since 'A' must have come from someone or something, let us then call that someone or something 'G'."

He added whimsically: "You know, like in that silly geometry — draw a line from point A to point G." He stopped, and still I made no comment.

"Mercy, lad," he said, "but you sure are not talking tonight."

"Father," I said, "Father Pat teaches composition and précis. You know I can précis what you have been saying in three words: God created man. Now, what about the Virgin Mary?"

"Father Pat! Sure I know he is teaching you English!" he said. "But can't you see, surely any fool can see, that God created man?"

"It is a pity that I am not one of them," I said. "But let us not jump to conclusions. I have no objection against your theory that 'A' must come from 'G'."

"Now you are talking," he said, and then went on: "And if 'G' is the very first and the very last of all, or in other words, 'G' does not come from anything else, and 'G' caused the conception of 'A', then what do you think of 'G'?"

I had nothing to argue on that point and kept quiet.

"No objection, and no admission," he went on. "Good enough. Now, Lert, tell me if 'G' can produce 'A' — we don't know how and what from, though certainly not from fusion of a man and woman, I ask you, what's to stop 'G' from producing Jesus Christ, in the same way, even though we don't know exactly how? Now you tell me, what's to stop Him?"

A few days later, I sat for the examination and as I had feared, I failed in English. Another year of hard work lay ahead of me, with more mathematics and more compositions to do. By the time the next examination was to take place, I was ready. I did not have to work late on mathematical problems any more. So one night, having nothing better to do, I dropped in to see Father Dan for a chat. He was busy as usual at his desk, correcting exercise books.

"Father," I said, "can I help you with those books?"

"Indeed you can't," he said, "and what would Father Rector be saying to me if I let you? God help me — but come, lad, and sit yourself down — here's a toffee."

He opened his drawer, took out a toffee and threw it over to me.

"Sorry, Father, to interrupt you," I said, and was about to walk out when he called: "No, no, sit down, can't you? And don't you bring me any more problems, because I still have more than 50 exercise books to correct."

"No, Father," I said. "I have no more problems...I'm only curious about the Holy Trinity."

Again the same thing had happened as before. Questions simply popped out of my mouth before I could even think of what I was saying.

Father Dan pushed away his books and turned to me.

"At me again with your problems, are you?" he said, and added: "Can't you let the Holy Trinity alone and let me be with my exercise books?"

I had to laugh, but a Jesuit is a Jesuit. He could no more leave theology alone than could I stop the questions from coming out of my mouth. He laughed, too, and we went at the problem in earnest.

We jumped from the Trinity to confession to the infallibility of the Pope, then on to the Eucharist and finally baptism. By the time we had started on baptism, it was 2 o'clock in the morning.

"On this matter of baptism, Father," I said, "do you think that my father and mother will go to hell if they are not baptized?"

"God bless their souls," he said, "but how could they go to hell, if they have a son like you? Mind you, I'm not saying that you are a saint, but neither am I one, for that matter!"

"Then, Father," I asked, "why should one be baptized in order to go to Heaven, while others don't have to?"

"Ah, now," he replied, "if I were God, I sure could tell you why I do this and why I don't do that, but then, you see, I am not God. Now, tell me, what do you think yourself? Will your father and mother go to hell?"

I could not tell him what I thought, for I was not able to think of any reason why anyone should go to hell. Then Father Dan said:

"So you are just an ordinary human being, who

think it's fair enough not to send your father and
mother to hell. If God is the origin of justice itself,
do you doubt His justice in dealing with the souls
he created?"

Then he added: "Jeepers, lad, but you really
do fight hard. Now instead of fighting Him, why
don't you try for once to drop your guard? Get
down on your knees and try to be friends with Him.
Be friendly yourself, if you want to make a friend.
If you do this, I tell you, He will come to you and
you will not be bothering me any more with these
problems. But now it's time for bed. Good night,
or rather, good morning, Lert. Now get some sleep."

The next day I could not possibly keep my eyes
open. I was asleep during the science class, and
Father Dan woke me with a rap on the head. I
went to sleep again during geometry class. He must
have shouted at me a few times, although I never
heard him, but the boy next to me woke me with his
elbow. Father Dan called me up to his desk and
wrote a note saying that I was to be punished by
staying in the study hall for one hour extra after
school.

I thought this was most unfair and entirely unreasonable. He knew that I had been with him till,
well, after two in the morning, and yet he purposely
punished me because I could not keep my eyes open.

That evening when school was over, I went to
the study hall and sat down at a desk. The hurt
and shame of it all overwhelmed me.

"How could he do this to me?" I kept asking
myself over and over again. But no answer came.
Father Pat, who was in charge of the study class,
came over to me and whispered, "What are you
doing here?"

"I am being punished for sleeping in class," I said.

"And who punished you?" he asked.

"Father Dan," I said and handed him the note. Father Pat looked at the note, crumpled it and said: "Well, I'm in charge here, so out you go! Didn't you stay talking with him until all hours of the morning?"

"Till nearly 3 a.m. Father," I said and could not keep the tears back. "I'm going to stay here till the hour is over."

Father Pat stood looking at me without saying a word. By this time the tears were falling incontrollably on to the desk, and I was miserable. Father walked quietly away. I said inwardly, "God, if I can't fight Father Dan, how can I fight you? I never really fought you, though I only wanted to know . . . Holy Mary, Mother of God, help me and pray for me, for I don't know how to pray."

Then I took out a pad of paper and started to write a letter to my father at home. The tears were still dropping down, this time on to the writing paper:

"Dear Father and Mother,

"I am going to be a Catholic. This is just to let you know about my decision. I might be wrong in not having asked your permission, but how can I ask for permission, when I cannot stop myself from becoming a Catholic. If I cannot, nobody else in the world can. . . ."

Father Pat must have been observing me all this time. He walked over to me and picked up the paper on which I was writing. He took a long time in reading it and at last, reluctantly, gave it back to me. He shook his head as if to say that he could not believe his eyes, could not believe what he had just read in my letter. Then he walked away. I finished my letter, addressed it and sat until the hour was over; then I stood up. Father Pat looked at me and nodded his permission to leave the room.

A month later, on Easter Sunday, I was baptized in the Cathedral and was confirmed on the Feast of Christ the King. As for my examination, this time I passed in the English subjects with no trouble at all, but failed in mathematics. Money did not buy me a doctor's degree in Hong Kong, but what I got, instead, was better than any money could buy —Faith.

Who am I to try and know God's mind, to question Him or even to tell Him that He should do this or that for me? Indeed, it is true, as written in the Book of St. Luke VIII, 18: "Take heed, therefore, how you hear. For to him who has, shall be given; and to him that does not have, even what he thinks he has, shall be taken away."

Nearly two thousand years ago, Jesus Christ cried out: "He who has ears to hear, let him hear!" And, by the grace of God, I have heard Him.

Note

BETTER THAN MONEY COULD BUY

[1] Nirvana is the goal of Buddhism, a state of "release" in which all desires have been extinguished. Whether it means also that the individual personality is extinguished remains unclear in Buddhist teaching. See the chapter, "Buddhists on Buddhism."

THE WITNESS

by Father John Shirieda, S.D.B.

The story of Father John Shirieda, S.D.B., is also the story of an Italian missionary, Father Adino Roncato, S.D.B., whose heroic death was reported in Japanese newspapers in 1955. He died while trying to rescue a student from a burning school building.

Father Shirieda is now rector of a seminary in the outskirts of Tokyo, where Japanese youths are preparing to become Catholic priests. He is also a professor of theology in Sophia University (Jochi Daigaku), Tokyo.

The "S.D.B." after his name means "Salesian of Don Bosco."

More than twenty-five years ago all of us, my mother, a sister and my brother, used to chant the ritual prayer to Buddha every morning on the threshold of our miserable dwelling. That prayer was an expression of our ardent devotion. In addition we used to present the prescribed offering of rice before one of his statues.

I have not included my father and I have referred to our miserable dwelling, because alas! the ravages of war had reduced us to a desperate plight. My father, a captain in an infantry regiment, had

60

died on the plains of China away back in 1937. Our home in Kagoshima had been reduced to rubble under the furious final bombardments by the Americans. The hope of finding a place of safety near our grandmother led us to move to a spot more than fifty miles from the city. But even here we found nothing but ruins and devastation.

For some years during the war, while anxiously following its progress, I had been thinking of taking my father's place by becoming a soldier like him, perhaps equally brave and more fortunate. The pressing need, however, in which my family was placed and the utter ruin into which the Japanese Empire had fallen dispelled these fanciful dreams. It was urgently necessary to rebuild our life on more modest proportions. I had to start with our home. There is plenty of wood in Japan and the undertaking of building a small dwelling appeared to be easy enough. . . .

But there were no nails!

A bright idea suggested by one of my companions showed me a way out of my difficulty. He proposed that I should steal nails from the stock of a Catholic church that was then being built with the aid of the American soldiers.

The thought of stealing was repugnant to me. But I was in extreme need. Furthermore, to steal from these hated foreigners, and Catholics into the bargain, must have appeared to me, in those days, as a good deed.

So, in fact, about midday, when all the workmen were taking their usual short rest, I made the attempt. Everything went off wonderfully well. I literally lined and reinforced my clothing with nails.

Cautiously I was making my way towards the exit when I thought: "I'd like to take a look inside the building." Curiosity overcame my fear. I climbed up to the height of one of the two windows and looked in. Just at that moment a priest inside, disturbed perhaps by the noise I made, looked up from his breviary and glanced in my direction.

I believe that a high-voltage electric shock would have had a less shattering effect on me. Before I could take thought, I was already running home as fast as my legs could carry me. With incredible speed, however, the priest was at my shoulders. I hoped to elude him, but our shorter Japanese legs cannot compete with those long Western ones. To make matters worse, I was laden down with the weight of the nails.

In less time than it takes to tell, I was already in the hands of my pursuer. I was trembling with fear. To fall into the hands of a white man, into the hands of a priest, and, above all, after such a disgraceful act!

Already I could see myself bound hand and foot and locked in a prison cell. Before my eyes came the picture of my mother, the mother who had given me the name "Masayuki," meaning "a just man" the mother who had taught me to be always scrupulously honest. It was terrible even to think of her learning about my theft and my betrayal of the hope and confidence she had always placed in me. So, while the priest was leading me back towards the church, I appealed to him, though with no hope, saying: "Do what you like with me. I ask only that you don't tell my mother!"

By way of reply the foreigner, when we reached the church, plunged his hands into the box of nails and offered me all I could carry. He then bade me goodbye, without saying one word about Christianity.

I made my way home utterly astounded, or rather convinced that I was having a fantastic dream. But in the hours that followed and during the whole night, I was haunted by the vision of the friendly face of that foreigner who had shown me an example of giving in that post-war period when we all wanted only to receive.

Next day I returned to the church in search of the priest. I found him and told him that I no longer wanted to become a colonel in the army. He had taught me, I said, that I should become like himself. Never would I have told him that he had taught me to become a Christian. Never! But in him I saw the Master-Teacher of Life.

That was the first of many frequent visits to the foreign priest. Later on, my sister accompanied me and still later, my brother also. Our faith in Buddha was gradually transformed into faith in Christ by means of that "witnessing" of the Christian belief.

Briefly, at Easter, 1947, my sister received baptism. In the following year, on the feast of the Assumption, the same walls that a few years previously had seen me entering cautiously to steal nails, now welcomed me amid the sound of joyous hymns. The same priest who as quick as lightning had caught up with me during my attempt to escape, now administered the sacrament of baptism to my brother and myself.

My mother remained an adherent to the worship of Buddha. In fact she threatened that she would not regard us as her children any longer. She used to say: "If you become Christians, you leave me; if you remain Buddhists, you stay with me." With time, however, influenced, no doubt, by our genuine and increasing affection and by the qualities of that priest "witness," much superior to anything else she had known, she became interested in this new mysterious religion. And to become truly interested in Christ is to be won over by Him, in spite of all difficulties.

We stayed together, even in subsequent developments. After our baptism my sister, my brother and I desired to follow our spiritual father in his vocation. In 1950 we entered the Salesians.[1]

In 1955 this same priest to whom I owe my life of grace and who awakened in me my priestly vocation, gave his life unhesitatingly to testify to his love for his Japanese brothers. In an attempt to save a friend of mine who was unable to escape from a burning school, he rushed into the blazing building. He died in the flames, his arms clasping the Japanese youth whom he was trying to rescue. He always used to say: "For love of Japan I would like to be consumed to the point of becoming Japanese dust." God granted his wish.

This fact strengthened me all the more in my vocation. I decided to become the second Don Adino Roncato — that was his name. In 1956 I was sent to Italy to meet his mother, who is now a second mother to me. I stayed there until I completed my studies in 1967.

At present my own mother is living alone in a country district in southern Japan, where she spends her whole day working for a small mission. My brother Anthony, a Salesian priest like me, is now teaching in our secondary school in Miyazaki. My sister Lucy, a member of the Salesian Sisterhood, is studying religious knowledge in their Higher Institute in Turin, Italy. As rector of the Salesian seminary and professor of dogmatic theology in Sophia University, I am engaged in the field of education for the priesthood. My sole aim is to model myself and others on that noble witness to Christ, Don Adino Roncato.

Note

THE WITNESS

1 The Salesians are priests, Brothers and Sisters of the Society of St. Francis de Sales, founded by St. John Bosco (1815–1888) and devoted particularly to the service of youth. Their founder, known generally as Don Bosco, chose St. Francis de Sales, one of the great masters of the spiritual life, as patron and model.

DOWN THE NIGHTS AND DOWN THE DAYS

by Thelma Wijenayake

Thelma Wijenayake is a Sinhalese, that is, a citizen of Ceylon, now the Republic of Sri Lanka. Her country, the picturesque island south of India, has a population of some twelve millions, of whom sixty per cent are Buddhists of the Theravada school. Buddhism came to Ceylon from India in the third century B.C. The writer is a resident of the capital, Colombo.

Mine was a rigid and orthodox background of Buddhism. If family tradition is to be believed, our line of descent on the maternal side goes back to the first two Buddhist missionaries to Ceylon, Prince Mahinda and Princess Sanghamitta, son and daughter of King Asoka of the Chandragupta dynasty. (King Asoka of India embraced Buddhism in the 3rd century before Christ.) The princess came accompanied by two ladies-in-waiting as befitting her royal status, and one of these, legend relates, is my maternal ancestress.

No one can prove the authenticity of this legend, but we do know that my grandmother bore a purely Indian name, Chintamani Boddhigupta, which is imprinted on her tombstone. She was Brahmin-like in her fidelity to vegetarianism, a fanatic in the way she upheld the sacredness of life. The faith of her fathers burned in her at a time when colonial rule was supreme and the Buddhistic way of life and its attendant culture were sternly discouraged by the British Raj—more, were even considered treasonable.

It is a matter of pride with us that our grand-parents and their ancestors did not sell their souls for a mess of pottage to curry favor with the British Raj but continued to practise their religion. They renovated their temple, built a new *vihara*,[1] and donated land, including rice-fields, to maintain the Buddhist priesthood.

So eager and vivid was their faith that when my grandmother died, they adorned her with her heir-looms of gold and consigned them all to the flames of her funeral pyre. The melted nuggets were fashioned into a statue of Lord Buddha, which holds pride of place in the *vihara*. When I asked my mother whether she regretted her decision to give up her share of jewels, she made a very expressive gesture, opening out her hands with the palms upward, and said: "My mother came bearing nothing and she has gone taking nothing."

The impermanence of everything was brought home to me then and it has never left me.

I am sure that my mother had a sixth sense and intuition that the spacious days of feudalism and pampering of children were at an end. When my father died, I was seven. He was an autocrat and sternly Buddhistic. He would never have coun-tenanced what my mother did. She chose the Roman Catholic nuns and a convent education for me.

To be transplanted from the warmth of one's home to an institution is an experience of heart-break and deadly sadness. There were other young

ones like me, our little selves heaving with home-
sickness, suffocated and half-drowned in floods of
tears. To us in our desolation there came a nice,
bright person, an Irish nun, Sister Honoria. She
pulled out largesse in the shape of sweets from her
capacious pockets, distributed them liberally and
said: "Now it's story time. It is the story of the
beautiful Mother. She is here with you. Don't you
cry." She had a lilting voice, a winsome face. I've
always been attracted to winsome people.

Good psychologist that she was, she knew how
we were hankering for our mothers. And so she
related the story of the beautiful Mother and her Son,
the Christ Child.

This, then, was my first contact with Catholicism. Being a dreamy type and vividly imaginative,
I was fascinated by this story and found comfort in
it as well. It has continued to appeal to me with
the passing years. "Now and at the hour of our
death . . ." It is comforting beyond measure to
know that she'll be beside me.

A child's mind is plastic and can be molded any
way the potter chooses. The convent years were
tranquil and orderly. There was no compulsion,
but I learned the questions and answers in the
catechism and all the Catholic prayers. I loved the
evening Benediction when Irish voices poured forth
their paean of praise and thanksgiving. I became
familiar with the melodies of Verdi, Gounod and
Schubert. My love of chamber music and the
classics was born then.

All this was a sentimental and emotional appeal,
for who is the child who could assess the pros and
cons of world religions? As was to be expected, I
asked permission from my mother, over and over
again through the years, to be baptized, but she kept

on saying a decisive "No." When I was eighteen, she relented somewhat and told me: "Decide when you are out of the sphere of influence of the nuns."

That day came. I was baptized.

I suppose it's an inexorable law of nature that impels a woman to fall in love. Love may lead her to forsake parents, home, even religion and God for the sake of a man, a comparative stranger who appears on her horizon. My life has been a departure from the traditional; it has never followed the set pattern. Only several months after my baptism, I met the man I was determined to marry, tall, dark, handsome but not of my creed or community.

In the fifties, when a Kandyan[2] girl wanted to marry a Tamil,[3] there was a furious uproar and families stood aghast. That was when I coldly, callously forsook the principles of the Catholic Church and put myself outside its pale by marrying the man I loved, in a civil ceremony. I considered the world well lost for him and lived in my fool's paradise for just a short while.

Punishment for my sin came quick on my heels. I lost two children — I who loved children so dearly. My mother died. The loss of a mother is the dissection of a part of one's being. I was bowed to the earth with sorrow. To defy God is to incur His wrath, (always accompanied by the offer of His mercy). Worse was to follow, when I discovered that my idol had feet of clay. The sordidness of promiscuous intrigues strikes deep into the roots of marriage, and what should be beautiful becomes soiled, distorted and ugly. It blasts marriage forevermore.

Should I have said, with Francis Thompson: "Is my gloom, after all, shade of His hand outstretched caressingly?"[4] I could not reciprocate even to God. I was frozen to my marrow. I did want it thus, to anaesthetize myself against pain. I would give Him back my allegiance but I could not muster any love or warmth.

Even a second marriage did nothing to disturb my zombie existence. It was a marriage of convenience to obtain a husband's protection to keep the wolves away. Church-going was automatic now. It was complying with a formality. A pale and anaemic relationship with God is a mockery, of little use. Perhaps the right type of priest could have helped to thaw out the ice encasing me and could have roused me to seek God's love. But an unfortunate occurrence prejudiced me against the clergy as being narrow, bigoted, suspicious.

When my second marriage was pending, I sought out a parish priest and gave him the gist of things as to who, what, where and how, and documentary proof pertaining thereto. At the second appointment there was a reception committee of four to interview me. It was a veritable inquisition no less, with cross-examination, imputing that I was lying to gain my ends. I did not like these men at all. I thought them hide-bound and lacking in sensitivity and delicacy. I was quite taken aback to find that priests who are supposed to major in psychology and deal so much with human nature should be found so deplorably inadequate when they came to assess an individual.

Contrary to popular belief, it is not always the melodramatic happenings that can influence one for good or evil. A simple incident that at first sight would hardly merit passing comment is often a milestone and a turning-point. Such an experience was mine when I walked into a church one Sunday.

On impulse I joined a queue outside the confessional, as there were only three in the line.

When I told the priest that I had not gone to church for almost twelve Sundays, I had schooled myself to hear the usual platitudes, the same stereotyped harangue about God's love and so on. How refreshingly different it was to be told instead: "Try giving a few minutes each week to God. Just to say 'Thank you.'"

Is this Rome's answer to the Space Age? wondered I. If so, he and his ilk would be a good contribution to this age and time, rather than the quartet I had met a decade ago, who were still mediaeval, apt to pontificate and inquisition-minded.

Strange but true that two sentences could bring about a whole trend of thought. Yes, I have always made it a point to say, "Please," "May I?" "Thank you," to all and sundry around me. How is it that I've taken God so much for granted, that I never extended even elementary courtesy to Him? I began to feel a mean ingrate — and so have kept my tryst each Sunday, not as a formality to be complied with but because I am convinced I want to say "Thank you," to God from Whom all good things come. I've heard it said that the young priests of today are unorthodox, unconventional, but what some would fain not realize is that these seeming rebels could, and do, have a depth of sanctity and a fervor that glows bright, sans compare, before their Master.

The priest of the confessional has the unique gift of being able to transmit his obvious love of the Eucharist to those worshippers who are present when he celebrates Mass. Devotion and dedication on the part of the celebrant do communicate themselves to the worshippers. He has helped me to care for

the Mass, to sense the sacred and mystic quality of
it. Dare I say now: "I love the Mass"? It has
been a slow and subtle process. First, I closed my
mind to the giving of whole-hearted worship. I
restrained feeling. The detachment sought and
fostered during a decade of years kept me free of
hurt. Hence I resisted and thought: "thus far and
no further." Literally, "I fled Him down the nights
and down the days...And in a mist of tears I hid
from Him."[5]

It was an unequal contest all along. I have
learned to give in with good grace.

Yet it is not that easy for me. Relics of the
Buddhist way of life and thought intrude on me.
Quiet and stillness for communion between God and
myself, especially after receiving the Blessed
Eucharist, is what I'd wish. I suppose it is the habit
of meditation and *sil* which generations of my folk
have practised. I like to see women dressed in
simple white when they come to worship, not in
ensembles, bedecked, bejewelled, posing and
posturing. These may be fine in a ballroom but
they are an affront in the house of God. The
humility of white-clad women is what I am used to.
Perhaps I should not allow myself to feel as I do,
but set patterns of life and thought implanted into
one are hard to eradicate. And Christmas, as it
draws to its tinselly climax, becomes a nightmare. I
begin to think with dread of the millions of living
creatures that will be slaughtered as food for the
saturnalia of feasting, so that the earth is drenched
with the blood of His own creation, and this is to
welcome Him! It is a paradox that I, for one,
cannot comprehend. With *Wesak* [the feast of
Buddha's birthday] they practise *ahimsa,* compassion
accorded to all living creatures, even to the meanest

and lowliest. Often I feel lonely in not having my people around me as I worship.

Have I, a Buddhist, found Christ completely, in His divine and human totality? One finds Him, and there is ever more and more to find in Him. It is not like stooping to find the gem that lies underfoot. It is more an unfolding, a quest, a long-drawn-out learning and seeking, often a groping in the dark, following glimpses of His light so that one eventually arrives. To indulge in emotions and transports of joy would be easy. We Asians are prone to it. We like steeping ourselves in ritual and ceremony. The Catholic Church has it, too — a resplendent altar, vestments, music, flowers. Coming from people who have never prevaricated with the truth, I do not want a spurious imitation, for emotion is but gilt on the surface. It has to be a deep and an abiding love for, and trust in, Christ. If within the past eight months I have rediscovered myself and have started thinking afresh, I hope that, by His grace, I know Him somewhat better now than before.

Notes

DOWN THE NIGHTS AND DOWN THE DAYS

[1] Buddhist monastery.
[2] Kandy in the centre of Ceylon was formerly a royal capital. The Temple of the Tooth of Buddha, one of the principal places of Buddhist pilgrimage, is located in Kandy.
[3] The Tamils are a South Indian people, many of whom settled in Ceylon in the second century before Christ and later. Most of them are Hindus, but there are large communities of Christian Tamils in various parts of South-East Asia.
[4] From Francis Thompson's best-known poem, *The Hound of Heaven.*
[5] From the opening stanza of *The Hound of Heaven.*

A DRY BONE IN THE DESERT

by the Most Rev. Ratna Bamrungtrakul

The writer was born of Buddhist parents
in Bangkok, Thailand, on February 11,
1916. His story up to his ordination as a
Catholic priest in 1949 is told in the following pages.

In 1969 he was named Bishop of
Ratchaburi by Pope Paul VI. In 1972 he
was chosen by the bishops of Thailand to
represent them in the Synod of Bishops in
Rome. He has written more than 20
books in Thai. His baptismal name is
Robert.

"Ratna will never be converted," said someone
of me, after having known me for three years as a
student in Wah Yan College, run by the Jesuit Fathers
in Hong Kong.

During those three years I was known to be so
completely indifferent to Catholicism that I hardly
ever set my foot in the chapel or ever discussed
religion. It was true that I learnt catechism, which
was part of the curriculum, but I seemed to treat it
as no more important than arithmetic or history, if
not even less. Perhaps it would have been much
better if I had serious objections against Catholicism,
for then there would be some opportunity for those
on the Catholic side to argue over the matter with

74

me and to convince me of the truth of Catholicism. But as it was, I seemed to be no better than a stone or a dry bone in the desert. And I was on the eve of leaving Wah Yan College, for I had passed the matriculation examination and was going to the Hong Kong University.

But a few days after I left Wah Yan College, a quiet ceremony of baptism took place in the Ricci Hall chapel, and the candidate to be baptized was myself.

Why then did I become a Catholic?

One thing I can say for certain: my conversion to Catholicism was due neither to the irresistible pull of truth nor the indisputable force of logic in favor of Catholicism. As I now look back on the succession of events of my school days, which included nine years in Assumption College under the Brothers of Saint-Gabriel in Bangkok, and three years in Wah Yan College with the Jesuit Fathers in Hong Kong, I cannot pin-point any momentous hour when my mind was so illumined by the light of Christian truth or so convinced by the irrefutable force of argument in favor of Catholicism that I had to say to myself: "Here is the truth, I must accept it. I must be a Catholic."

How then did my conversion come about? I was baptized in 1937, at the age of 21, on the eve of entering the University of Hong Kong. A young lad of my age and in such circumstance is usually furiously proud of his own power of reasoning, and I surely was no exception, as could be deduced from the fact I had joined the Debating Society in Wah Yan College and had enjoyed arguing on every possible subject, except, of course, religion.

I think I had better reserve the answer to the end of this brief sketch of myself. For the moment

I would describe the course of events which contributed toward my ultimate conversion.

I would not hesitate to say that my father, a fervent, sincere Buddhist, was indirectly responsible for preparing the ground for the growth of the seed of Catholicism. He possessed the natural virtues in a quite remarkable degree. He neither smoked nor drank. He was very thrifty, hard-working, honest in all his dealings, generous to his neighbors and friends, pious in his religious practices, and bore malice towards none. All his friends held him in great esteem. He had no prejudice against Catholicism. When a Catholic friend of his died, he did his best to help in the solemnization of his funeral. Although nobody would call him a holy man, he was so regular in practising the normal religious observances that his fidelity earned him the greatest respect from his neighbors. Every morning he would be seen seated at the gate of the house giving food to sixty or seventy monks. This went on until he was too old to do so and was crippled by partial paralysis.

He trained his children in the strict observance of virtues. They were taught to do all kinds of work, even the humblest, to be thrifty, and exact in manners. Because of his example I never smoked nor drank and was contented with only a small sum of pocket-money. I worked side by side with the servants in the house and served at table when my father invited his friends to a banquet. These good habits were so deeply engraved in my character that I found no great difficulty in practising them later.

It was my grandmother, however, who taught me to say the Buddhist prayers and to give food to the monks. Although my father prayed every day, he never obliged his children to do so, but he strictly observed the Chinese New Year together with all the rites and celebrations. I grew up in a home which could be called typical of the middle-class Buddhist home of a businessman.

At the age of seven I entered Assumption College in the French section, as all my brothers did. I studied there for nine years. During this long period I never had any interest in Catholicism, and it never impressed me as being attractive and worthy of special consideration in any way. I considered it as one of the many religions in the world. I rarely set foot in the Cathedral except on some funeral occasions.

There are, however, two small incidents which I particularly remember. One morning when I was playing with some friends of mine in the playground, I met Brother Martin de Tours, the Director, in the corridor. There was nobody around. He stopped me and with great zeal began to speak about Catholicism for a short while. I listened attentively and respectfully, and then rushed off to play, without being in the least impressed by what he had said.

During one of my last years in Assumption College we were taught a little of Catholic philosophy. The Brother who taught us tried to prove the existence of God by logic. I listened but I was never conscious that I was particularly impressed or convinced. But then neither was there any serious doubt in my mind, which seemed to be in a state of stupor in regard to Catholicism. I was not attracted by it, nor did I object to it. I was completely indifferent.

I left Assumption in 1932 with my heart full of love for my Alma Mater, of admiration for its system of education and training, and of respect for all the Brothers and teachers.

A few months later I sailed for Hong Kong to

join one of my brothers who was studying in Wah
Yan College. He had gone there only the year
before.

In Wah Yan College I continued to be completely indifferent to Catholicism. Of course I had
to learn catechism, as it was part of the curriculum;
but the Catholic doctrine somehow never seemed to
impress me at all. I remembered having entered the
school chapel only once, on one Christmas night and
listened to a sermon by Father Gallagher, then the
Rector. I could not remember being impressed by
his sermon in any way. In fact I went there just
because my brother asked me to. Otherwise I
would never have set foot in the chapel at all!

My brother was one year with me and then
returned home.

While I was in Wah Yan College I was very
fond of reading storybooks. Sometimes Father
Bourke, the Warden, went out of his way to comply
with my wish to get books to read. I was grateful
to him for his kindness but never gave him a chance
to approach me in matters of religion. Father Ryan
also tried to get contact with me by asking me to
draw maps for his monthly magazine, *The Rock*.

One day Father Ryan came to my room to ask
me to draw a map. He casually remarked: "Aren't
you interested in religion, Ratna?"

My answer could not be briefer. "No,
Father." The subject was dropped as suddenly as
it was introduced.

I saw some of my friends become converts and
receive baptism. But my curiosity was never
aroused. I considered religion as a personal affair.

Father Martin, then a scholastic, used to take
us out for hiking during weekends to the seaside or
up the hills. I loved the scenic beauty of Hong

Kong, and enjoyed those hikes very much. But I never talked to him about religion. I took part in all the school activities, except the religious ones.

Then something began to happen.

During my last year in Wah Yan, while I was preparing to sit for the Matriculation, Father Donnelly arranged a retreat in Kowloon for us.

"It would be a good thing to make a retreat before you leave school," he told us. A number of students, both Catholics and non-Catholics, expressed their willingness to go. Out of class spirit I decided to go, too, having only a very vague idea as to what a retreat was like.

The retreat was held in an old school building in Kowloon, roomy, quiet, with a garden to walk about. I did everything just as every retreatant did. One thing I still remember is that I was very strict with myself in keeping silence throughout the retreat. I saw no vision, and received no special illumination that I was conscious of.

When the retreat was coming to a close, Father Donnelly had a brief talk with each retreatant individually. He had one with me, too.

"How do you like the retreat, Ratna?" he asked me, smiling.

"It's good, Father," I answered.

"What do you think now about the Catholic religion?" he asked.

I said that I still doubted about some attributes of God. He tried to explain. I nodded, and left him as usual, without being much impressed by his words.

Apparently I remained as indifferent to Catholicism as ever before. I myself was not conscious of any change in me which would indicate that I was thinking of becoming a Catholic.

But there *was* a change.

Later a friend of mine mentioned it to me. "You know, So-and-So (a non-Catholic) said that when you came back from the retreat, you were a different man," he said.

Now I realize that I was different. There was a kind of joy, a lightness of heart that had never been in me before. I smiled and laughed with a kind of happiness which seemed to fill my heart. I was really happy, spiritually happy. No wonder some of my close friends could not fail to notice the difference.

A drop of divine grace had soaked through the thick rampart of indifference in my heart, and somewhat quenched its thirst for truth and happiness to which it naturally inclined. Color began to appear on the faded petals of the soul. The dry bone in the desert began to show a little sign of life.

All this was accomplished so quietly, so secretly, in my soul that I was not even conscious of it.

As if drifted by a gentle current of grace, the ship of my will had entered the harbor of the Holy City, the Catholic Church. Night had imperceptibly given place to day; the fog began to lift, showing to the eye of my soul a glimpse of the spiritual world. The divine hand had touched my heart, and the contact brought a gleam of light and life into my soul.

Now there remained only an opportunity for the hidden light to manifest itself to my consciousness and to others.

After the retreat I continued to behave in the same way as before; outwardly there was almost no difference at all.

After I had passed the Matriculation and

prepared to leave Wah Yan to go to stay in Ricci Hall, I went to see Father Bourke, the Warden, for the last time, to pay the bill and to say goodbye. Father Bourke, perhaps rather saddened that I had been under his care for three whole years without any apparent benefit from the religious influence, remarked casually:

"Ratna, you would be much better if you were a Catholic."

Suddenly I burst out, "Yes, Father, I want to remarked casually:

Father Bourke must have had the greatest surprise of his life. The subconscious acceptance of Catholicism, like a mighty torrent, burst through the rampart of indifference, and swept it away altogether once and for all. A heavy load seemed to drop off my breast, I felt relieved, light-hearted and happy.

A few days later I was quietly baptized in the Ricci Hall chapel. Father Ryan performed the ceremony and Chevalier J. M. Alves was my godfather.

I deserve no credit for becoming a Catholic. Grace, and grace alone brought me into the Catholic Church. *"Gratia Dei ego sum id quod sum.* By the grace of God I am what I am."[1] I had defied all human attempt to convert me, but I could not resist the impulse of divine grace.

It is true that the goodness of the Brothers of Saint-Gabriel and the Jesuit Fathers and their excellent system of education had done much to prepare the ground for the seed of divine faith which in due time would be sown in my heart.

But the question is not so much the "why" and "how" I became a Catholic, as the "why" and "how" I remained a Catholic. I knew some who were converted but did not persevere in their faith.

Humanly speaking, I would face the same difficulty
in keeping the faith as they did, but somehow I
managed to persevere to the end.

That was due to the transformation of my life
after baptism.

Formerly I was completely indifferent to
Catholicism; now I was furiously eager to know
everything about it. I did not want any question
to remain unanswered and any doubt to remain
unsolved. Now I spared no effort in finding how to
explain satisfactorily the teaching of the Church. I
wanted my faith to stand on firm foundations of
reason and logic. I studied Sheehan's Apologetics
and Ripley's *Radio Replies* several times over. I
studied Ignatius Cox's Ethics, with the kind help of
Father Byrne. Chesterton, Belloc and Maurice
Baring became my favorite authors. My interest in
reading now turned completely to religious subjects.
Marmion's *Christ: the Life of the Soul,* St. Thérèse's
The Story of a Soul, Goodier's *Saints for Sinners,*
John Farrow's *Damien the Leper* became my
favorite spiritual books. I became a member of the
Apologetics Group and in 1941, our Apologetics
team of Ricci Hall won the cup in an Apologetics
Bee against the Sodality of St. Joan of Arc.

The more I studied Catholicism, the more I was
overwhelmed by the completeness of its explanation
of the problems of life. For me it became the
foundation of all other branches of knowledge. I
took delight in noting the harmony between science
and Catholicism. I was amazed to find how the
Bible proves to be the key to understand the history
of mankind, how the Catholic Church can help to
solve social problems, and offered the only adequate
defense of morality and even decency, how she
enthusiastically promotes art, science and progress in

all branches of social activities. I searched out all the current objections against the Church and found her refutation complete and satisfactory. I think that I was so critical of the teaching of the Church that if her teaching were not completely true, I would not have remained a Catholic for long.

I became a daily communicant, was admitted into the Sodality of the Children of Mary on May 29, 1938, served Mass daily and found real pleasure in adorning the altar of Our Lady during the month of May. I took an active part in running a stall in the Saint Vincent de Paul Bazaar, and in securing old clothes for the poor. The spirituality of St. Thérèse, the Little Flower, impressed me deeply and I tried to imitate her.

What a transformation from the state of complete indifference which had hung over me for more than twelve years of close contact with Catholicism! Grace seemed to have swept me irresistibly on and on. I told my father of my conversion and he raised no objection, perhaps without realizing how much my new religion would mean to me.

When I graduated in May, 1941, and the road of success opened wide before me, I decided to become a priest.

I returned home with the hope that my father would hear my plea and give his consent. He not only would not grant my request but tried to persuade me to give up my faith. He was quite surprised and angered in finding that I was so fervent in the practice of my religion. The time was just after the war with French Indochina, and the Church was going through a hard time. Reasonably enough from his point of view, my father was anxious lest my profession of Catholicism bring the whole family into disrepute. He could not understand why a

Catholic should be so "stubborn" in his religious belief and practices.

I realized that my faith had become a source of distress to everyone at home and there was practically no means to make them understand my position. I was now facing the crisis of my life. I had to choose either God or the world.

Strengthened by the Blessed Sacrament, received at the Carmelite Convent which stood just close to my house, one afternoon I left home, forever, without saying farewell to anyone, without any word or any note as to my destination. I entered the Seminary at Bank Nok Khuek, in Ratburi, just before the war in the Far East burst out in full fury. While the war was going on all around us, in that quiet corner in the midst of a thick coconut plantation, disturbed only a few times by the sounds of bombing, a group of seminarians, and I among them, studied philosophy and theology. I was ordained on the feast of Saint John Bosco, January 31, 1949.

Note

A DRY BONE IN THE DESERT

[1] This saying of St. Paul the Apostle, himself a convert, is from his First Epistle to the Corinthians, chap. XV, v. 10.

BUDDHISTS FIND CHRIST

A TEACHER'S STORY

by Ursula Boonsom Charoen-eng

The writer is an educator, teaching in one of the leading schools for girls in Bangkok.

"Don't let them persuade you to become a Catholic," my headmistress smilingly warned me one day when I went to pay her my usual visit.

I was twenty-three years old then. She was the headmistress of a famous college in Bangkok where I had completed the teacher's training course. It was she who sent me to the Mother Superior of Mater Dei,[1] who had asked her to choose one of her best students to teach there.

For nearly two minutes I was silent. I was baptized already! I did not want to conceal the fact that I was a Catholic. Why should I be ashamed of being a child of God? Is it not a great honor to show that I am a Catholic?

At last I broke the silence. "I am a Catholic, Madame," I said, looking confidently into her face. This short answer made my heart light. I did not think that I had done any wrong.

The smile faded from the face of the learned old lady. With an exclamation of surprise she leaned back and looked straight into my eyes. "You are a Catholic!" she said softly. "I am sorry ... but I have known you long enough. I

85

have confidence in you and feel that you must have some good reasons for changing your religion." She ended by saying again: "I am sorry..."

The words, "I have confidence in you and feel that you must have some good reasons for changing your faith" have always rung in my ears. I thought that if I wrote the story of my own conversion, it might make others understand our Catholic faith — and me — better and realize that I am a Catholic not because of somebody's persuasion but by the grace of God, the grace to know Him, to love Him and to serve Him, the grace that has given me spiritual happiness.

I have always remembered the first day I came to Mater Dei. It was in May, 1940. In the small and rather dark room connected with the chapel, on the wall opposite the entrance, there hung an oil painting of a Man crowned with thorns. Some drops of blood stained His face, weary and suffering, but His eyes still shone with the light of love... the love I need and shall always seek.

In that moment, while awaiting the Mother Superior who would receive me to be a teacher there, I had a strange feeling in my heart. It was my first step on my spiritual journey.

I was nineteen years old then and the younger daughter of my family. I had been separated from my father since I was about twelve years of age. I lived with my mother, who did her best to support me and provide for my education. The broken and divided home made me sad. I still felt the need of fatherly love. I had only one sister, who married a good man. Later, when she learned that I was baptized, she regarded me regretfully.

After about a year as teacher in Mater Dei, among the Catholic nuns, teachers and surroundings,

I found myself interested in the Catholic religion. I saw those around me praying and enjoying their work. It seemed to me that they were happy. I was not thinking yet of going so far as to change my faith. I only wanted to know the truth.

One morning I went with my Catholic friend to Mass at the Calvary church. After that I went frequently. It was during the war. At that time Catholics in the remote parts of Thailand were persecuted. Seeing that I always went to the Catholic church, my mother was very worried. So I stopped going there but I still felt the need of "something" that would make my soul happy. I went to the Buddhist temple to ease my mother's worries, but I could not find the "something" that I needed. I did find the difference between the practice of the followers of these two faiths.

I longed for fatherly love, for calm and happiness of soul. Where should I find them?

The kindness of God, the heavenly Father, never ended for me. . . .

In October, 1942, Bangkok was flooded. I had some important school work to finish, so I decided to stay in the school, with the permission of my mother and the Mother Superior.

After one month in Mater Dei as a boarder, I completed my work. During those days I went to Mass in the chapel of the school every morning and studied the catechism with the Mother Headmistress. The most important thing was that I found the real light of happiness, so I decided to be a Catholic.

When the flood was over, I returned home and took the first opportunity to ask my mother to permit me to be baptized. Sadly she gave me permission. It seemed to her that I, as a Catholic, might be separated from her!

The Mother Superior of Mater Dei fixed the day of my baptism. It would be the 6th of January, 1943, the feast of the Epiphany. But my obstacles had not yet ended. About one week before that day I fell seriously ill with malaria and my grandfather died. So my baptism had to be postponed to Holy Saturday.

I should have three days for retreat to prepare my soul before baptism. So I asked permission from my mother again to stay at school. She did not permit me but scolded me for asking. She did not understand that to be a real Catholic I had first to learn the doctrine fully. After seeing me cry the whole evening, she reluctantly allowed me to stay in the school as a boarder in preparation for baptism.

At last I was baptized — by the grace of God. Thanks to His kindness, I found real love and happiness of soul amid the suffering and trials of life. I wanted my mother to share it, too.

After eight years of prayers, my mother was baptized in the chapel of the Salesian seminary of Hua Hin. Now we are both Catholics. We join our hearts in prayer and rejoice in the love of Our Lord, the real and eternal God, and under the protection of our heavenly Mother.

Will those who read this story of my soul please pray for my sister and her family that they may one day find this real happiness, as we, mother and I, do?

Note

A TEACHER'S STORY

1 Mater Dei is a school for girls conducted by the Ursuline nuns in Bangkok.

A DOCTOR'S QUEST

by Dr. Chiang Shu-wen

The writer was born in North China
and studied medicine in Peking and Nanking. He is now an ophthalmic surgeon
practising in Taipei, Taiwan.

My name is Chiang Shu-wen, 62 years of age,
born in the prefecture of Fong-cheng Hsien, in the
province of Antung in mainland China.

I come from a Confucianist family. We preserve our age-old tradition of the worship of Heaven,
respect for Confucius and veneration of ancestors.
My parents were not Buddhists, though they did
observe the abstinence from eating meat on the first
and fifteenth days of the lunar month. This was my
family education, and I had no contact with Buddhism in my childhood.

At the end of my secondary schooling, my
classmates and I went on an excursion to Liao-yang
prefecture in the Chie-shan mountains, where there
are many Buddhist pagodas and Taoist temples. We
stayed for three or four days in the pagodas. There
I saw the furnishings, the vestments, the paintings,
the statues and the Buddhist ceremonies. I spent a
long time watching and reflecting on them. All at
once I experienced, unexpectedly, a very deep sense
of the utter vanity of this world here below and
everything in it. A great sadness overcame me.

I went to the bonzes[1] to ask them their reasons for giving up the world and leaving their families. I learned that there were bonzes who had really studied Buddhism and were convinced by it, who practised virtue and were believed to have reached a very high level of learning and asceticism.

In reality, there are two distinct categories among the bonzes, the higher grade which comprises the intellectual bonzes, convinced and practising believers, and the lower grade that includes those who engage in material administration and dealing with the outside world. In the latter group are those who have entered because of poverty, to get a living. There are also men guilty of great offenses who have come seeking asylum, for in olden times it was the custom not to inflict further punishment on any offender, no matter how great, once he had taken refuge in the pagoda and had his head shaven. The emperors regarded him as having left human society and as dead to this world. But most of the lower grade have come to be admitted as bonzes because they have failed in their political, professional or financial activities or in love affairs. By this experience they have discovered the uncertainty of this world and so they have taken refuge in the "door of futility" to seek deliverance there.

These bonzes of the lower grade can be promoted to the higher one, if they can progress diligently in the study of Buddhism and can put their learning into practice. In Buddhism all are basically equal. Everyone can become a Buddha if he practises virtue. The sixth Patriarch of Chinese Buddhism, Hwei-nen, could read no Chinese characters and did not understand what the fifth Patriarch, Hung-jen, preached at all. But once arrived at the stage of illumination, he was able to give out all the authentic teaching of Hung-jen, clarify it and develop it. That is how he became the sixth Patriarch.

Such was my first contact with Buddhism.

After graduation from my secondary school, I went to Peking for higher studies. Questions about the meaning of human life were coming into my mind more frequently now. I could not forget Buddhism. The doctrine of the equality of all living beings appealed to me greatly. I admired and relished Buddhist proverbs, poetry and literature in general. Peking was the centre where the most celebrated bonzes and the great Buddhist scholars of the day were gathered. Thus I was able to have contact with the Reverend Tai-hsü, a bonze known all over China, who used to explain the "Book of the Forty-two Chapters." I went to hear him speak at length. I can still recall some of his very striking sentences, like the following:

> "One is bound to one's wife and family more than to a prison. The day comes for leaving prison. The year to leave one's wife does not come."

I went also to hear another course of lectures in which the Buddhist Books were expounded by the bonze Chang-hsing, who explained them rather from the philosophic point of view. During this period I convinced myself vaguely that one should have a religion but I took no further step.

One day I visited a Catholic church and I even asked for the loan of some books to study. I was told that the books could be lent only to those who sincerely wished to become Catholics. Catholicism seemed mysterious to me.

I was studying at the army medical college, the dean of which was a Protestant. We had no class

on Saturdays. Our dean invited a Protestant minister
to come and preach to us about the Gospel and to
get us to study the Bible. Since I did not understand much of what he was expounding to us, I did
not make any serious study of Christianity .

Afterwards I went to Nanking, where I often
attended the conferences on Buddhism given by a
professor of Chin-ling University, Mr. Mei Kuan-hsi.
In his talks he used scientific terminology so that the
public could understand him better.

Frequently, too, I went to Protestant churches,
seeking there the solutions that would deliver me
from my inner disquiet, for I was in a very distress-
ing spiritual condition. Nobody was able to satisfy
me. Consequently I placed all my confidence in
Buddhism, regarding it as the principal religion that
I would profess and hoping to find in it true deliverance from my sufferings and thus the interior peace
I craved. It was then that I had more contact with
Buddhism.

As well as the books on medicine that were
necessary for my profession, I was accustomed to
read the Buddhist books as a matter of duty. I liked
them so well that I regarded them even as recrea-
tional reading. I did not concern myself much with
my family nor thought about it, for, according to the
teaching of Buddhism, all that — wife, children and
family — is something truly extrinsic, exterior, to a
man, just as wealth and property are, and constitutes
an obstacle to the practice of virtue and to achieve-
ment of enlightenment. One should renounce all
of it.

The Sino-Japanese war broke out, however, and
in my soul another struggle began to take place.
My patriotism obliged me to reconsider my faith in
Buddhism, for in the face of aggression by a hostile

power, if one wishes to save one's country, one should have a true patriotism and be ready to sacrifice everything for this cause. The doctrine of "no killing" would let us be killed by our enemies, and when it preaches the vanity of everything, it implies that national sentiment and patriotism are also vain. The fact is that in Southeast Asia all the Buddhist countries became colonies of the Western powers or at best retained only nominal independence; China must look to Buddhism for one of the main reasons of its national weakness in the past.

This basic idea led me to discover gradually, one after the other, the defects and shortcomings of Buddhism. Chief among these are the following:

1. *It is scientifically defective:*

I have studied medicine; everything has to be proved. Now the facts related in the Buddhist books cannot be considered as having a historical basis. They are only myths—for instance, the three lives of the individual, metempsychosis (the transmigration of souls). . . . All these doctrines are very important but they cannot be proved from either the scientific, historical or theoretical point of view.

2. *Impractical doctrine:*

To become, some day, a Buddha (an Enlightened One), which is the ideal of every Buddhist, one should pass from the Three States or Conditions, the state of passion, the state of form, and the state of formlessness. One should deliver oneself from this impure and evil world. But how can one rid oneself of this world, since one is obliged to live in it?

3. *Too abstract and mysterious doctrine:*

The Buddhist books are innumerable. In the literary sense they are well written or translated, but they are too difficult to understand. One finds oneself utterly unable to study them in depth. Perhaps the doctrine is too elevated, but it ought to be within the reach of everybody in order to save everybody. In Buddhism the Chuan[2] sect is the most highly esteemed. In it people hope to have "illuminations," enlightenments, by means of meditation. But the method of meditating is sometimes so absurd that one finishes by setting it at naught, and the "illuminations" are sometimes so "elevated," as they say, that the people cannot grasp them. One can only set them aside.

4. *Inconsistencies and contradictions:*

In Buddhism there is great insistence on the principle of "not killing." One day I went to the famous bonze Tai-hsü (already mentioned) and asked him: "We, medical doctors, take great care to have harmful bacteria killed. Would Buddhism permit us to do this?"

After long reflection, Tai-hsü gave me this answer: "Killing these bacteria, which are harmful to mankind, will not constitute a sin against the commandment of 'not killing.'"

I said nothing further, but where is the principle of the equality of all living things? How could one claim that there is no contradiction between "killing" and "not killing"?

Another example: Lamaism is one of the sects or forms of Buddhism. Every year the Lamas celebrated the feast of Beating the Devil in the Yung-ho Palace in Peking to drive away the evil spirits and to invoke blessing for the people. One of the instruments they use in the ceremonies of "beating the devil" is the celebrated whip made of human skin. They preach "not killing" and use this sort of whip. There I see inconsistency.

5. *Cold indifference:*

Compassion is a very important virtue in Buddhism. But this compassion is, to my way of thinking, something rather cold. It is practised with a certain condescension, with the idea of an alms being given and at the same time a certain humiliation for the recipient.

All these motives, and possibly still more that I cannot now recall, are very personal and may even seem to be of no great importance in the eyes of others. But they made me withdraw in disagreement from Buddhism, and thereafter I went no more to the pagodas and paid no visits to the bonze.

The thought of the vanity of this world, however, and the question of the meaning of life always kept coming to my mind, especially at the time of my arrival in Taiwan. I was not very busy in the hospital where I worked. Reflecting on the past and looking towards the future, I felt my whole being overwhelmed with the sense of uncertainty and anguish. I reached the conviction that I had need of a religion in which I would find spiritual rest.

One day, going along Chung-chen Road in Taipei, I saw the Shan Tao Temple but did not go in, because I was no longer interested in it. Farther on, I caught sight of the Catholic church of Hwa-san. I should have liked to go in and request some information about religious matters, but I decided by preference to write a postcard to this church to ask about the possibility of getting instruction in Catholicism. Probably it was by Father Fang, then the parish priest that I was introduced to Father Joseph Kung, who took charge of instructing me.

I was delighted to meet Father Kung, who made me acquainted with the Catholic religion, and after some time I decided to ask for baptism. This was indeed the religion I wanted.

Allow me to tell what I have found in Catholicism as compared with Buddhism.

1. Everything that Catholicism affirms or preaches has always a philosophical reason or a historical or theological proof.

2. Catholicism has a doctrinal consistency, without contradictions or merely gratuitous assertion. There are mysteries in it that one cannot comprehend, but you are told clearly and sincerely where the mystery is that surpasses human intelligence. You are given the reason why a Catholic accepts this mystery while leaving others their freedom to make their own decision.

3. You are given a manual, a handbook of catechism, with which one can progress at one's ease, learning the truths to believe, the commandments to observe, the sacraments to receive and the prayers to say. Everything is clear, not as with Buddhism, in which one does not know where to begin, because of its multiplicity of books and its diverse sects.

4. The Catholic priests preach with the authority of the Church, which has received the command of Christ to go and teach all nations. By whose authority do the bonzes "preach on their thrones"? What are the norms that they should observe? What is the criterion of their orthodoxy? I only see that the bonzes praise and uphold one another or they themselves display their own talent without any mission from on high. In Catholicism I have found an assured basis for religious belief.

5. Catholicism preaches God's infinite love, which not only humiliates nobody but on the contrary uplifts the believer in every respect, strengthens him, and makes him confident, with complete aban-

donment to God, in all the circumstances and difficulties of life. Thus he can live with a sense of assurance.

6. Catholicism calls on one to practise faith, hope and charity. People in the West who have been educated according to tradition through these virtues, become imperceptibly more active, more courageous and optimistic not only in religious affairs but in regard to life as a whole. They are ardent, with great zeal for the development of science, the extension of knowledge, the reform of society, help for the poor and the progress of mankind, because they are educated in the spirit of these three theological virtues.

Face to face with the sorrow of human life and with this sinful world, Catholicism has no thought of running away from either. It tries rather to remedy them, to understand them and to turn them to good. It is as if a house was on fire; the Buddhists rush to escape through the window or the door or any exit, while the Catholics try to enter the house to extinguish the blaze. Or again as if confronted by a house in ruins, Buddhists want to tear it down completely but Catholics think rather of repairing it and improving it so that people can live in it.

8. The Popes of various periods have always encouraged their flocks to love their fatherland, to build up their country and to become part of society in order to understand it, to uplift it, to sanctify it and to save it. Buddhists are anxious to be rid of it. Their ideal is to go off into the most distant mountains.

In short, I became a Catholic and turned away from Buddhism just because, thank God, I had been able to observe the two religions at length and to compare them. Catholicism has given me sound reasoning, proof and the way by which one can save society, one's country and one's soul. I have been baptized now more than twelve years. I am sorry that I have not progressed more than I have in religious knowledge and in the practice of virtue. But I am happy to be a Catholic. I have had my whole family baptized and when the occasion presents itself, I bring our holy religion to the attention of my friends and colleagues.

Notes

A DOCTOR'S QUEST

1 Buddhist monks.

2 This is known in Japan and elsewhere as Zen. It originated, apparently, in China during the 8th century.

BUDDHISTS FIND CHRIST

HEARING GOD'S CALL

by Michael Phan-Huy-Du'c

Professor Phan-Huy-Du'c is prominent in educational circles in Vietnam. He is the founder and principal of the Lycée Cu'u-Long, a private secondary school in Saigon. He is a past president of the Federation of Private Schools (Écoles Libres) of Vietnam and represented the Federation at the 5th International Congress of Private Schools at Bad Godesberg in 1959. He has also held administrative posts in the government and in 1967 was elected as deputy in the National Assembly. He has written extensively on educational and economic questions as well as on religious subjects. He is a Knight of the Holy Sepulchre, holding the rank of Commander with Grand Cross.

Lord, if my Confucianist father has taught me to be Christian, if my mother, president of a Buddhist association, has taught me to be grateful to the Blessed Virgin,

if my Communist sister has taught me to have respect for the social justice taught by Christ and His saints, and if my Taoist uncle has taught me to place their true value on the goods of this world,

if thanks to them I have a better grasp of Your

laws, grant to them, O Lord, Your salvation, because every light from Your Wisdom should contribute to bring the totality of Your love to man.

*   *   *

I always loved the sound of the bell ringing from the pagodas to mark the watches of the long night, to hail the break of dawn or to call men, before the rising of the moon, to evening meditation.

As a child I experienced a strange resonance in my soul from that bell. I felt drawn towards it, mysteriously distant or clear-sounding, as towards a friendly voice.

When my grandmother was dying, my father asked for prayers from the pagoda of Thien-An that she might enter Nirvana.[1] He told me this on his return from his daily visit to the hospital of Quang-Ngai where he was chief physician. As yet I understood nothing about Nirvana, but my childish mind sensed that to liberate, to help a soul, one prayed. We spent that night in the pagoda. When my father went to be with the bonzes at prayer, I slipped out of my bed to join him. I saw him in the dim light of the candles, amid the smoke of the incense, bowed down in the deep recollection of a son who ardently desires happiness in the Beyond for his mother.

The bonzes chanted in unison with my father to the rhythm of the rattles alternating with that of the gongs. All this harmony created an atmosphere both spiritual and mechanical. Everyone kept the cadence and stopped precisely at the signal of the rattles and gongs. As the night went on, the chanting rose in volume to reach and impel Buddha.

Staying in a corner, behind one of the pillars of the pagoda, I entered into this devout atmosphere and felt transported into a realm above the earthly.

After that, for my grandmother's happiness, I kept to the vegetarian diet on the first and the fifteenth of the lunar month, that is, to the Buddhist fast. It meant, in my time, eating rice with salt mixed with a little pepper. Times have changed. The modern Buddhist fast allows a comparatively rich fare; even "chicken" is eaten — that is, cooked lotus-root, seasoned with pepper and tasting just like chicken.

I kept to this rule even during my three years as a boarder in the Quoc-Hoc school in Hue. When I went to the school of the Brothers of St. John Baptist de la Salle, I took a strong stand against their teaching, particularly during the half-hour of catechetical instruction.

I sought to oppose the Brothers in the matter of doctrine. What upset me most was the possibility of the Brothers' compromising with the conquerors of my country, the French. The idea of Christians as traitors was embedded in my mind. Reading the documents sent by the missionaries to the Empress, wife of Napoleon III, seeking help, confirmed me in this thought.

As a boarder with the Brothers from 1929, I was enabled to relish the beauty of the Christian liturgy. The Mass, solemnly celebrated, captivated my mind and heart. The more I felt attracted towards this religion, the harder I found it to tolerate the idea of disciples of Jesus coexisting with partisans of foreign domination.

One day I put this question point-blank to Brother Ignatius, who had charge of my class.

"If we are at war with our conquerors, on what side will you be?"

"I will fire on them," the good Brother answered unhesitatingly.

This quick reply made a strong impression on me, all the more because in his daily life Brother Ignatius was in no way combative.

Relieved on this score, I continued my inquiries, drawn in turn by the influence of my Confucianist father, my Buddhist mother, my Taoist uncle, and, above all, my sister who had very advanced ideas on the social question.

Claimed by the Buddhist ideal which passionately seeks to kill all passion, by the Confucianist program which seeks to elevate man, and by the Taoist which is an Oriental form of Epicureanism, I felt myself inclined, however, towards Communism which offered a more down-to-earth, realistic program, that of leveling all social inequalities by force and establishing equality in well-being by maintaining this force. The blood pulsing in my veins, my very youthfulness, would choose the direct method, strong measures.

Force has always captivated the young. Dictatorships find their best partisans among them.

These thoughts agitated my soul. My thinking, however, became more mature through my attendance at daily Mass.

If the idea of force appeals to the young, they find still more appeal in the sacrifice of Him Who, all powerful, offers Himself up to satisfy Justice.

This God Who teaches through parables, Who heals the deaf, gives speech to the dumb, pardons the adulterous woman and enlists fishermen for His mission, took hold of my soul. When from the centre of the sanctuary the Mass-servers rang their bell for the elevation of the Host and chalice, I bowed down in adoration of Him Who loves. . . .

In our daily work I observed, with satisfaction, that those pupils of my class who applied themselves with sustained effort were always ahead. Theirs were the highest marks and the highest places. The success of Lanh—today a Redemptorist—made me appreciate a new factor in the making of our own happiness: our will.

Lanh's schooling began when he was thirteen years old, having been a boy herder of buffaloes, like the other youngsters of his village, up to that age. He learned just enough Chinese characters to sign debt papers. (Buying on credit has been a practice in Vietnam from time immemorial, but the people speak of debts rather than credit.) But Lanh was fortunate. Instead of sending him to the village scholar who taught classes seated with his pupils on a mat, his parents sent him to the primary school. He rose through the classes with the result that he entered the Brothers' school. Here this peasant boy would take two hours to learn a lesson for which others took only half an hour. During the times of recreation and in the dormitory he kept on learning. Nobody paid attention until the day when the marks were announced. He came first. The smarter pupils protested; the lazy ones waxed sarcastic.

Thereafter, the idea of establishing equality in well-being by force carried less weight with me. Even supposing that all the proletarians of the world succeeded in overthrowing order everywhere, in suppressing all capitalists and in taking their place, and in leveling everything, Communism could never reduce the efforts, the intelligence and the wills of all to one level. So revolution would have to be recurrent, endemic. My youthful mind weighed the simple facts and found the fallacy in the Communist solution to the problem of human welfare. In practice it would be impossible to solve this problem by process of upheaval. If we wished to maintain the effect, a new world revolution would be necessary after every two or three generations.

To satisfy this rational being called man is a complicated matter.

When I was reciting the Buddhist prayers, the chants in the Sanskrit language lulled my mind without satisfying my heart. To annihilate all the passions means annihilating oneself to some degree. That was repugnant to me. The attitude of Buddha compelled my admiration but did not win my adherence.

I continued, however, to observe the Buddhist fast on the first and fifteenth of the month, while assisting every day at Mass.

One day Brother Alphonsus made me a present of a little book entitled "History of the Saints for Every Day in the Year" and a prayer-book for youth. I read the History of the Saints every day, on the eve of each saint's feast. At morning Mass I was reminded again of the saint in the commemoration. I became less reticent during catechism class. The prophets who prepared the Jews for the coming of the Messiah prepared me to accept the words of life.

These were prophets who were consistent throughout the centuries in heralding more and more clearly the coming of Christ, until their prophecies were crowned by the definite words of the Annunciation. This consistent continuity impressed my youthful mind, appreciative of the marvelous. And was not a life that, in one respect after another, conformed with the prophecies, truly marvelous, this life of God made man?

"Why," I asked, "did Our Lord not lift up the

cross, He Who could still the tempest? Why did He carry it, dragging it along?"

"Our Lord did not wish to use His divine power," I was told, "because He was to redeem us by suffering. He wanted to express His love. Having become man, He bore the cross as a man, so that my sins and your sins would be atoned for and pardoned."

This dialogue took place between Brother Ignatius and myself during the Holy Week retreat of 1928. Our good Brother Director Aglibert Marie read the Gospel of the Passion for us. He spoke quietly, but his voice trembled when he said that it was because of his sins and ours that the good Jesus died, died ignominiously. . . . Sitting in the wide courtyard, we joined him in weeping with the women following the Blessed Virgin to Calvary.

"Blessed Virgin, help me to love Him who has so much loved me."

During Holy Week and Easter of that year, on leaving the refectory, I would kneel before the statue of Our Lady of Victory, who is also Our Lady of Lavang,[2] begging for light and asking her to help me to get my father's permission to become a Catholic.

My three brothers and I wrote to our father to request this permission. After persevering with these letters for three months my brothers gave up, in the face of my father's emphatic refusal. I alone continue to write every day. At length, one week before the Feast of the Immaculate Conception, 1929, Brother Anselm received a letter from my father permitting me to become "a Christian not merely in name but truly a Christian."

My father, who could recite by heart from the Epistles of St. Paul and could appreciate the beauty of the religion of Chateaubriand, recognized the

divinity of Jesus Christ, but as a filial son he would
not give up ancestor worship. He accused the
priests of having reduced the divine religion of Jesus
Christ to dimensions that suited themselves. He
could not see how in a religion in which after the
three commandments devoted to God, the fourth en-
joined filial piety, the ceremony expressing gratitude to deceased parents could be forbidden.[3]

For a long time this was a problem of conscience
for him. Yet unknowingly he had steered me towards Christian ideas. Habitually he would quote
the Gospels and St. Paul to me.

On receiving his letter, I wrote back to thank
him. He did not reply. My sister answered in his
stead and congratulated me on having realized my
wish. She had come out of prison, where the Sûreté
— the security police — of the French Protectorate
had put her because she had led the students' strike
when the leaders of the Vietnam Quoc-Dan-Dang
(nationalist organization) were executed. I was
very fond of my sister. To her I directed all the
affection I had for my mother, whom I had lost at
the age of four. During the eight months of my
sister's imprisonment I offered all my actions,
thoughts and prayers for her liberation. With tears
I recommended her to the Blessed Virgin, praying
that the police would not persecute her.

I did not know yet what it is to undergo torture,
but my imagination pictured it as something terrible
for a young girl. Somebody assured me that Sogny,
the head of the security department in Central Vietnam, was not in favor of torture. He was able — I
was told — to convince the revolutionaries and win
them over to the cause of the Protectorate. This
assurance did not quell my fears; I continued to pray
with perseverance and confidence. After eight

months in prison, my sister was set free on the feast of the Holy Name of Jesus.

All that is still vivid in my memory, and my eyes fill at the thought of the motherly consideration shown by the Blessed Virgin. She heard my prayers, led me to the interior life, guided and upheld me.

Wrapped in thought, one day, I did not see one of the Brothers approaching. I had to hurry. It was meal-time. The other pupils had finished washing their dusty feet and were on their way like a flock of sparrows, leaving me behind.

"Michael!" A sharp slap made me see stars. "You are happy now? But why did you get Brother Anselm to write to your father?"

"He is my teacher."

"Yes, your former teacher. Couldn't I ask permission for you?"

That slap made me realize clearly what it costs to go ahead in the religious life. To the Blessed Virgin I offered this introduction to mortification.

One must do something to merit the faith, a free gift.

I understand the wrath of the Brother, who that year was my mathematics professor. He was very devoted to his pupils. He was displeased with me because I had acted through Brother Anselm without consulting him. But his displeasure went no further than the slap.

In spite of my four years with the Brothers and the six hours a week of catechism and the daily quarter-hour of reflection, I had to question the good chaplain, Father Kinh, during catechism class.

"Why do the Vietnamese priests have recourse to the French authorities to win lawsuits?" I asked him.

"All the Vietnamese priests do not have recourse to the French to win lawsuits. . . . Look at me, for instance."

We began the first catechism period with this exchange and we always ended with some reflections on Franco-Vietnamese relations. I would have won the approval of my father and the whole Phan family, which from 1884 has included patriots of real worth who died in the dungeons of Poulo-Condore or on the scaffold.

"One can be a Christian and Vietnamese at the same time." This thought sustained me and I prepared for baptism with my mind at ease.

I assisted at Mass with greater fervor and made my spiritual communion with devotion. The booklet, "Visits to the Blessed Sacrament" by St. Alphonsus Liguori, opened up before me the infinite treasures of the Eucharist.

Incapable of comprehending the immensity of God's love, I had recourse to the Blessed Virgin, begging her, my heavenly Mother, to do what I could not — to perfect my acts of love.

What shall I say of the happiness that flooded my soul on December 8, 1929? I chose this day, feast of the Immaculate Conception, for my baptism. In going through the Lives of the Saints for Every Day I had decided on Saint Michael the Archangel as my patron. For me he was the symbol of faithful love. His great name, meaning "Who is like unto God?" appealed to me.

When the purifying water of baptism flowed down my forehead, I felt plunged in happiness. It was a calm joy. a feeling of peace, of spiritual poise, of hope . . . and of the actual nearness of God.

I was sixteen years old, but my feeling was of childhood. Is not Christianity, which renews the youth of the spirit, the outpouring of immortal youth?

All along the spiritual pathway that led me from Buddhism to Catholicism I saw how God in His infinite goodness puts salvation within the reach of everybody.

Other religions give precepts; none of them has given the means of fulfilling them. In place of a "static" religion, Catholicism presents a dynamic one, offering to man an energy, a daring, and an extraordinary power of conceiving and achieving spiritual aims.

God offers man the sacraments: Baptism, regenerating the soul; Penance (confession), purifying it regularly; the Blessed Eucharist, ever increasing its union with God; Confirmation, fitting him to be apostolic; Anointing of the Sick, helping him in the ordeal of grave illness; Ordination, which empowers those chosen to continue the ministerial priesthood; Matrimony, the sacrament of marriage, which Jesus Christ honored at Cana, when He began His public ministry.

The sacraments tell the soul, enveloped in the Christian life, that God is there.

"Now, young Trappist monk, better learn your lessons! That's more pleasing to God now."

The voice of Brother Cecilius roused me from my daily reading of the lives of the saints. I was neglecting my lessons and thought only of becoming a monk. My comrades Lanh and Chuyen had gone to enter the preparatory school of the Redemptorist Order.[4] They had chosen the better part. That evening I was reading the life of St. Bernard, who led his whole family towards the monastic life. Should I imitate him? I was the only Christian in our family. Perhaps I should draw back a little from the shore, like Jesus in the boat, to be better heard. . . .

That year I failed in my examination.

My father, angered, took me out of school. Thereafter I spent my time praying, preparing myself for the religious life, and for two years I never ate a full meal. Every evening I joined others for prayers in the little church of Faifoo,[5] which then had no resident priest. I went to Danang — then called Tourane — for Mass at Christmas. A Redemptorist priest gave the sermon. After Mass I told him that I wanted to become a Redemptorist. The superior of the Trappists had decided not to accept me.

Just before Têt (the lunar New Year) my father received a letter from the priest requesting permission for me to go and teach in the Redemptorists' preparatory school. My father guessed what was in my mind.

"Do you want to join the Order?"

"I do, but it is very difficult. I cannot meet the requirements in education, health and so on."

He allowed me to go.

Father Larouche, Canadian, welcomed me in Hue.

"They tell me that you engage in politics," he said. "That would create a delicate situation for us, since we are foreigners here." The pioneer Redemptorists in Vietnam were all Canadians.

"I can't do otherwise," I answered. "And I am convinced that Vietnam Christianized will be a great Vietnam."

He assigned a companion for me. I shared the life of the "Juvenists," the young candidates for the Order. I was in raptures of happiness. But after a month I fell gravely ill and returned to Faifoo.

The Redemptorists and the Juvenists prayed hard for me. In Faifoo, with no priest near, I seemed to be dying. My sister, a non-Christian, traveled 22 kilometers (more than 13 miles) to get a priest for me, lest I should die without the last sacraments. I received them on the feast of St. Joseph — and regained consciousness. My father rejoiced. In his thirty years practising medicine he had not seen such a recovery. The coffin he had already bought for me became a token in honor of St. Joseph.

During my illness my father told me: "My dear boy, I know that you would recover more quickly if I became Christian. But who then would carry out the worship of our ancestors?"

My aunt and then my eldest brother were baptized. They were followed by the wives of two other brothers and by one sister, who later became a nun, a nursing Sister in Montreal.

It took me two years to regain my health. I returned to the Redemptorists' school, no longer as an aspirant to the religious life but as simple monitor or prefect. I stayed there for thirteen years.

During that time Father Larouche enabled me to fulfil my desire to complete my studies.

My father recognized the kindness shown towards me by the Redemptorists.

"Duc is right in saying that the Fathers love him more than we do," he said. "They love him for the love of God, while we sometimes scold him for our own sakes."

I learned more and more about Christian spirituality, profiting especially from a book of Eucharistic devotion by St. Alphonsus Liguori and the teachings of St. Thérèse, the exponent of the "Little Way" of spiritual childhood. The more deeply I pondered on the interior life, the more I appreciated the sublime calling of the priest.

"I am sad," I told my confessor, "because I cannot become a Redemptorist."

"What? Do you seek to be a Redemptorist or to do God's will? My child, perfection consists in doing the will of God."

To find out more clearly what God's will was for me, my spiritual director and I made a novena. On Christmas Day, 1938, he advised me to marry Marie Anne Tien, whom I had recently met again after a long interval, to find that our esteem for each other — both Catholics — had grown into love. Father Larouche officiated at our wedding and consecrated us to the Sacred Heart in the Church of Our Lady of Lavang.

In spite of the dangers and hindrances of recurring warfare and harassment by several regimes, we succeeded in bringing up and educating our twelve children.

One memorable crisis was the almost fatal illness of our daughter Felicity. The doctors said that there was no hope for her. My wife and I prepared to accept whatever God's will might be, but prayed, through the intercession of the Blessed Virgin, Mother of Perpetual Help,[6] that, if He saw fit, He would cure our daughter for His greater glory.

She recovered, against all human expectation. Her Buddhist grandmother, my step-mother, her eyes fixed on the picture of Our Lady, said, in a trembling voice, that it was miraculous. "All your life you must be grateful to the Blessed Virgin" she told us.

Eight years later, she herself lay dying. She was president of the Buddhist Association in Dalat. On her deathbed she asked to be baptized.

Notes

HEARING GOD'S CALL

[1] See footnote on Nirvana in the chapter, "Buddhists on Buddhism."

[2] The church and the shrine of the Blessed Virgin Mary at Lavang, in the countryside north of Hue, in Central Vietnam, constitute a centre of national devotion. Here, according to tradition, Christian refugees were favored with Our Lady's protection in a time of persecution.

Catholics believe that Christ, the Divine Saviour, hears all prayers, even those of sinners. But He responds most readily and most generously to the intercession of Mary, the holiest of His creatures, whom He chose to be His Mother. Furthermore, He made us adopted children of hers, giving us a claim on her motherly care and giving her a mother's right to plead for us. Hence Catholics ask her confidently to intercede for them, while they honor her because she is so near and so dear to Christ.

[3] In Asian countries some of the traditional ceremonies honoring the dead were associated originally with superstitious beliefs. Hence Catholics were required not to practise them. This was to avoid giving any impression of compromise or inconsistency and to safeguard the young Christian communities against doctrinal confusion.

In the course of time, however, it became clear that many of these ceremonies and customs had lost whatever connection they might have had with forms of worship or superstition. They had become simply expressions of filial reverence or civic respect, in which persons of all religions or none could join. Accordingly Catholics nowadays are free to honor the dead with any ceremonies or observances that are not evidently superstitious or otherwise contrary to their faith.

4 Redemptorists are a worldwide body, the Congregation of the Most Holy Redeemer, founded by St. Alphonsus Liguori (1696–1787).

5 Faifoo in Quang Nam province in Central Vietnam is where the first permanent Catholic mission was established in Vietnam, in January, 1615. It is known more commonly today as Hoi An.

6 "Our Mother of Perpetual Help" is a title by which the Blessed Virgin Mary is widely known and venerated, and her intercession sought, by Catholics in Vietnam as in other countries.

LIGHT SHONE IN A PRISON

by *Augustine*

Once a novice in a Buddhist monastery in Burma, the writer continued his spiritual pilgrimage as a university student and an army officer.

Born into a Buddhist family, he entered the monastery at the age of fifteen, like other Buddhist boys, for a short novitiate. During it he received intensive religious instruction and followed the monastic rule. After that he completed his secondary studies and then entered the university. He reacted to his first lessons in biology by becoming skeptical about his religion and veering towards atheism. Proficient in English as well as Burmese, he was an avid reader of H. G. Wells, Thomas Huxley, George Bernard Shaw and others like them. During his student days he read some Christian literature, too, but it had little, if any, effect on him. Delving again into Buddhism and Hinduism, he sought illumination and spiritual power by practising meditation and self-control. His efforts seemed to be fruitless.

A journey to England gave him no religious inspiration. As a strong Burmese nationalist he entered military life. Burma had regained her independence in 1948 but

115

soon afterwards faced a revolt by the
Karens, one of the peoples constituting the
Union of Burma. The writer served in
the Burmese army and was taken prisoner
by Karen forces.

At that point he begins his narrative.

One morning in mid-1950 I found myself alone
in a cell of Toungoo prison in a state of great distress. Like my comrades who had attempted a jail
break during the night, I had received beatings and
bootings from the prison staff. We were Burmese
army officers who had been captured in battle by
Karen rebels in February, 1949, and had already
been in the prison for about a year and a half. Now
the Karen officials had decided to put us in solitary
confinement as punishment for the attempt to escape.

On reflection, I thought that this was an
excellent opportunity to undertake a strict regime of
spiritual exercises as prescribed in Buddhist religious
texts. Once before I had tried it during a summer
college holiday at home. Though I persevered then
for about six weeks, I did not achieve any degree of
the spiritual advancement described by the venerable
author. But this time I would have twenty-four hours
of undisturbed peace every day, for an indefinite
period, to pursue my spiritual goal.

I felt encouraged. Of course one could not
expect to go very far, but even at an elementary level
there were clearly defined stages to assure one that
he was on the right path.

I prayed and said many beads of the Buddhist
rosary. Many times a day I sat for an hour or more
to meditate on particular aspects of religious truths
contained in the Abidhamma, the metaphysics of

Buddhism. During these meditations I also carried out the Anapana Kamahtan, a breathing exercise somewhat on the same principles as its counterpart in the Hindu yogas.

I had read that two weeks' practice of the Kamahtan had brought some people to achieve Samadhi, a state in which all their faculties are absorbed on a spiritual plane, leaving them oblivious of their surroundings. On the other hand, many failed to reach this stage in a lifetime of perseverance. The explanation given was that people of the former class had accumulated great merit in their previous existences, while the others had no such spiritual credit accruing from their past. Buddhism in our country believes in reincarnation of the individual repeated innumerable times, in different forms and states of existence, not only human but also animal and even on levels lower and higher than either.

The Burman never forgets that some day he will die and that material wealth will be of no avail but will only drag him down to hell all the more quickly if he has not reached a certain stage of spiritual development. This he can do by religious exercises, by spending his remaining years in a monastery (which also means giving away his possessions), by donating as much of his wealth as he can to the poor or by self-sacrifice in the service of others. He can then hope to attain, in his next existence, a life that he can devote wholly to religion and thus get started on his way to Niekban or Nirvana.

During our captivity all of us Buddhists performed our religious exercises very seriously. I spent much of my time on them. But usually after meals I passed an hour or so reading. One of the few books available was the Bible, a King James

version, kept in prison offices for swearing people in.
I had also a Buddhist religious text, which one of
the prisoners, a criminal, had given me. It was a
standard work by a venerable abbot; it contained the
same fundamental teachings that I had once studied
in a monastery.

At the end of every religious exercise I prayed
to Superior Beings, whoever or whatever they might
be, to help me to attain enlightment and to ensure
that I was on the right path. I was particularly
conscious that the Buddhist Dhamma, as we knew it
then in Burma, could have acquired accretions from
a variety of sources such as Hinduism, spiritualism,
animism, astrology and the cultural traditions of the
different groups that make up the Burmese people.
I knew, in addition, that there were many interpretations of the Dhamma given by distinguished Buddhist
abbots and lay exponents.

I persevered in my religious exercises for some
months. I did not seem to make noticeable spiritual
progress other than having complete peace of mind,
an attitude of charity towards all my fellow-beings,
my enemies included, and a contented conscience.

Time was of no importance, however. I harbored
a patient hope that I would be fortunate enough to
achieve at least an elementary degree of spiritual
advancement before anything disastrous would
happen to us.

Many of the rebels who held us prisoners were
extremists. Should they suffer a severe defeat—day
by day the government forces were growing stronger
—we could not expect to be spared.

Among us army officers in captivity there were,
as well as Buddhists, two Christians and one Muslim.
The Christians were Anglo-Burmans, one a Catholic,
the other an Anglican. While in solitary confine-

ment, the Catholic officer made persistent demands
that a Catholic priest be allowed to visit him regularly. A Catholic priest was likewise requesting
permission to visit him. After a couple of months,
the Karen authorities gave way. One factor in this
development was the influence of a fallen-away
Catholic among the rebel leaders. Though Baptists,
these Karens were rigidly sectarian; they looked
down on people of any other sect or religion. They
were afraid, however, that if their Catholic prisoner
died without the ministrations of a priest, it would
be a great calamity not only for him but also for
those who had obstructed relations between him and
God.

Consequently a missionary priest of Toungoo
was allowed to visit him every week. We all bene-
fited by these visits, for our Catholic fellow-prisoner
shared with us the books that the priest brought him.

To me he sent books and magazines of general
interest. I wanted something more. As I had great
difficulty in understanding the religious ideas in the
Bible, especially the Old Testament stories, I asked
him to get me books that would explain how Christians can accept God as described in the books of
Moses and by the Prophets. I found parts of the
Old Testament rather fierce as religious reading,
although God's great attributes of love and mercy
were also made clear in it. To us Buddhists it was
a fund of great sagas. The stories fascinated me,
and I felt deep sorrow for the Jews of old. But
the story of Jesus in the Gospels was even more
appealing. I found the simple, direct account of
His life and teachings very touching. It sounded
like a faithful documentation. But, of course, being
good Buddhists, we all felt that the Gospels had
nothing to do with us in our own lives.

Furthermore, having studied science in the university and having read popular books on the subject and English socialist writings and even some of Marx and Lenin, I felt unable to accept the idea of revealed religion.

In response to my request my Catholic comrade sent me some Catholic books. The first I read, if I remember right, was the autobiography of St. Thérèse of the Child Jesus. The second, I think, was *The Story of Jesus* by Ronald Knox, a synthesis of the four Gospels, with footnotes and explanations of customs in Palestine at the time of Jesus. This book helped me considerably to understand the message of the Lord, His messianic mission among men and the reason why Jewish leaders rejected Him. It made me think more seriously about the meaning of the Gospels. I was deeply moved by the personal tragedy and the simplicity and self-sacrifice of Jesus, narrated so sensitively in Ronald Knox's book. But I found the promise of salvation to believers in Jesus Christ rather too naïve as religious dogma. We had been brought up in a complicated set of religious ideas. We had always been taught that every man must work for his own enlightenment and that there was no short cut to Niekban or Nirvana.

Accordingly, undisturbed by my reading and my thinking about Christianity, I continued my daily Buddhist exercises and prayers.

But with more reading my interest in Christianity grew. I came to realise that there was a vast difference between Catholic beliefs and those of the Protestant sects. I was shocked that there could be so many sects for so simple and direct a religion. I wrote short notes to my Catholic fellow-prisoner, about my inability to believe, and he got some substantial literature for me from the priest. Thus I was able to read the *Confessions* of St. Augustine, short biographies and accounts of St, Thomas Aquinas, St. Francis of Assisi, St. Thomas More, and books of apologetics by Archbishop Sheehan and many others whose names I have forgotten. I was greatly impressed by the book, *Radio Replies,* a collection of answers given by Father Rumble of Australia, who dealt with queries and controversial issues in his broadcasts.

After reading these works and pondering carefully over the doctrines, I began to understand the nature of Revealed Religion. Whereas formerly I had rejected such ideas out of hand, I was now able to appreciate the value of the message of the Bible.

Even so, I was still unable to believe. I found Christianity foreign to our way of life. The customs and life-style described in the Old Testament seemed strange to our civilization. And because Christianity was the religion of the colonial rulers, the British as well as other Europeans, I had unconsciously associated it with the evils of imperialism. Hence my spiritual progress towards Jesus was hindered by my national sensibilities and by Hindu-Buddhist ethical concepts.

At the same time I felt that there was much truth in what Jesus taught. "If only I could believe," I would tell myself, "the certainty of salvation would be open to me." Still this inner struggle was not such as to disrupt my Buddhist religious exercises.

As I read more and more, I felt that I could believe in Jesus Christ and love Him. But Christianity as a whole, its heritage of Judaism, the Old Testament, the civilization of the modern nations that had accepted Christianity, and many other aspects of the Christian world had become seemingly insurmountable obstacles to my seeing Jesus as my Saviour.

It was after about a year's study that I felt able to accept all the Catholic dogmas. I had read some Protestant books also. But the Catholic writings seemed to me more consistent, more thorough in examining theological issues, expressive of a stronger faith and offering a surer guidance. I felt that if I were to become a Christian, I would be a Catholic rather than spend a lifetime trying to work out my own private theology. I decided that if I accepted the Gospels as being on the whole quite genuine, all the assertions of Jesus contained in them must be taken as truth. In the circumstances I thought that the Catholic dogmas of the true Presence of the Body and Blood of Jesus in the Holy Eucharist, the authority of the Apostles and their successors, and the Sacraments were quite acceptable.

The most appealing part of Catholic life to me then was the great self-sacrifice of the Catholic religious orders, their spirituality, their dedicated labor and self-denial, and, of course, the heroic sacrifices of Christian martyrs under the Roman empire. Still I had no faith in Christianity. I was only intellectually involved with the Catholic doctrines and perhaps emotionally moved by the history of Jesus.

I think, too, that in the subconscious mind there lurked the idea that the God of Israel, of the Old Testament, though awe-inspiring and inflicting chastisement, was also a mighty God Who was loyal to His people. The thought of the Almighty keeping His promise to His chosen people was one of the realizations that responded to my spiritual needs just then.

I never ceased praying for light and never gave up my spiritual exercises. I felt sure that I would receive guidance sooner or later.

The year 1950 was drawing to a close. I knew that Pope Pius had proclaimed it a Holy Year. I wrote to my Catholic fellow-captive, asking him to pray to Our Lady of Fatima that we might regain our freedom before the New Year. If we did, I would believe. (I had read about the message of the Blessed Virgin Mary given at Fatima in 1917.) At the time I did not understand what grace is or how it operates, though I had read the theological textbooks studied only by seminary students and had also read what saints had written about the grace they received. In any case I made a promise one morning to the Blessed Virgin that I would become a Catholic if she would obtain for us the miracle of freedom before the year's end. Meanwhile I did not curtail my daily Buddhist exercises.

Later I felt that I had been presumptuous in asking for freedom in exchange for conversion. I was like the people in the Gospels who demanded that Jesus would work miracles at their bidding to give additional proof that He is the Son of God.

Instead of satisfying my presumptuous condition, God answered by allowing further misfortune to befall my officers and me. Christmas came and went with no improvement in our lot. In the New Year the Karen rebels suffered a heavy defeat outside Toungoo and they decided to withdraw.

One night the prison warders told us to get up and come outside. They then lined us up at the prison wall. I thought that our last moments had come. I was not at all agitated. I was quite satisfied that I had done my best to improve my spiritual state. After a while the prison officials came with two Karen military officers. They had decided to take us with them in their retreat and to hold us in the hills as hostages.

Tied hand and foot, we were brought by truck through the darkness to the largest Karen village in the eastern hills. On the next night we were taken to another village, a small and primitive tribal settlement. Here we were herded into a new prison, a freshly built bamboo stockade. In it there was no solitary confinement. We were all together and we could talk freely and enjoy each other's company again.

I told my Catholic fellow-captive of my problem with the Old Testament. He advised me to read the Psalms. I took his advice and was captivated by the Psalms, which I read daily. The adoration and love of God, so beautifully expressed in them, enraptured me. My friend had also with him the *Imitation of Christ* by Thomas à Kempis. During my days of solitary confinement I had had the loan of this small book of great spiritual value but only for a short while. Now I could read it every day. This book, with the Psalms and the New Testament, stirred and elevated my thoughts. But I was still not a Christian.

About six days after our arrival, the guards and villagers took us out, a few at a time, to bathe at a spring in the valley. Most of us were back inside the prison by evening, when the villagers came up to the stockade yelling angrily at us. The local guerrilla leader shouted that a prisoner had tried to escape and had been shot in punishment. Now we were threatened with the same penalty. The village leader brandished his revolver, saying that the people had debated whether to shoot all of us but had decided to starve us to death instead.

As the senior officer among the prisoners, I replied that we had nothing to do with the escape. The hapless man who had made the attempt was a civilian pawnbroker, imprisoned because he refused to tell where he had hidden the gold in his charge. But the village strong man was hysterical, shouting that if he had his way, he would shoot us all. We kept silence.

After a day of total starvation the Karens relented. We were given one meal a day, but with a reduced ration of rice. A few days later the area commander of the Karen troops came and apparently told the villagers that we were prisoners of war and should be treated with some legality. After that we were given two meals a day but only very small portions of inferior rice. Some of our number gave a little of their own rations to others who were in great need.

Time passed, and again it was the Christmas season. Our warder asked us to sing Christmas carols for the villagers and thus to build up some goodwill among them. There were now three Christians among us. Our Catholic fellow-prisoner took the lead and coached us all in the carol singing. On Christmas Day we sang from inside the prison. We were told that the villagers appreciated our gesture.

After Christmas some Baptist and Anglican pastors, Karens, visited us and tried to console us. The Anglican pastor was particularly kind. Later on, the wife of a Karen officer came and held a prayer meeting with some villagers inside our prison. A collection was taken up and she turned it over to the warder to buy meat for us. From this beginning she organized a prison charity once a month. Then the warder suggested that we should make coolie hats from bamboo leaves to sell to the farmers. We made them, and the proceeds were used to buy food. Relations between the villagers and ourselves improved.

During this period I began to say the Catholic litanies as part of my daily prayers. Even before that I came to wear the badge of the Sacred Heart of Jesus.[1] It happened this way:

I had a gold ring with a red stone, given to me by my elder sister when we were in college. Sewn into my vest, it remained hidden from the warders. Now as my friends badly needed meat and tobacco, someone appealed to me to sell the ring for the benefit of all. In place of it, my Catholic comrade offered me his Sacred Heart badge. The ring had been given to me for luck. He explained that the prayerful wearing of the badge was a powerful invoking of divine protection. I had read about devotion to the Sacred Heart of Jesus while I was in Toungoo prison. Seeing that the sale of the ring could do some good, I gave it up and from that day I wore the Sacred Heart badge around my neck. After wearing it for some time, I began to pray to Jesus and to say the Rosary[2] rather than my Buddhist prayers.

Slowly I became convinced that my prayers to the Superior Beings, asking for guidance to the truth, were being answered in a subtle way. I found that all my trials and sufferings were a preparation for me to become a Catholic. My conviction was growing stronger that God does exist and that Jesus is the Christ, the Son of God. Step by step I came to believe in the Holy Trinity. I prayed daily that we would be freed so that I could receive baptism.

I knew that among Catholics May is traditionally a month of special devotion to Mary, the mother of

Jesus. I decided to make a novena to her during
that month, praying that through her intercession we
might obtain our freedom soon. I offered prayers
daily through her, recited extra Rosaries and said all
the litanies I knew, including hers.

On the fourth and fifth days of my novena two
messengers from our Government troops arrived,
disguised as itinerant hawkers going from the low-
lands to the hill villages. After dark they made
contact with one of the prisoners through the bamboo
palisade and formed plans. They were to return to
Toungoo and bring back enough men to help us to
break out of prison and lead us to safety.

A week later, around midnight, our would-be
rescuers came and blew open the lock of the prison
door with a hand grenade. But the consequences
were sad. Shooting began, in which two of the
rescuers were killed. One of the prisoners was
killed and two wounded by the grenade. Others were
killed later by the villagers.

We followed our rescuers out, but they were
only six and in the dark of the monsoon night my
group lost contact with them. I had three men with
me, including the two wounded officers.

For three nights and two days we wandered
around in the rain-shrouded mountain country without food or compass. On the third day we stumbled
on a group of Karen women working in a field. They
called out to their men, who came quickly with
guns. We were too weak to do anything but
surrender.

We expected to be killed on the spot. Instead,
we were treated very well. Our captors gave us
rice, brought us to their village—one of them carried
me—and put us in a hut near their church. The

village elders, the Baptist pastor and wives of Karen officers came to see us and gave us good meals.

After a day or two we were moved to a hospital in a large village that had become the general headquarters of the Karen revolt. Here we were joined by two of our own who had also escaped and been recaptured. We checked each other's stories and found that six of our men had been killed.

To me the saddest news was that of the death of our Catholic comrade, my spiritual benefactor and a friend to all who met him. Though he did not try to escape, he was shot in cold blood. He was a very brave man, who would give no thought to his own safety if he could help others. As an army officer he was able, resourceful and quick-witted. A brilliant chess and bridge player, he was an entertaining companion in the most hopeless situations. He was a man of utter faith, entrusting all his burdens to Jesus and never worrying unnecessarily. I felt that he should have escaped or survived, but one cannot penetrate God's designs.

In my escape and while wandering on the mountainside, I carried my little bag containing the Bible and other religious books. All the time I continued to pray. Now in the hospital I was helped by Baptist and Anglican pastors, all Karens. They lent me religious books. One gave me a New Testament in Burmese, a beautiful leather-bound edition. The Karen nurses looked after us as if we were their relatives.

After about six weeks our health had improved, wounds were healed, and we were moved into a hut outside the village. Our lot was better now than before our attempted escape. But it was not freedom, and worse might befall us if the Karen rebels were to suffer more serious reverses. At the end of the monsoon rains in mid-October the Government troops were likely to launch an offensive. The rebel forces would probably have to withdraw. In that case they might move us into more primitive hill areas. We learned that already the Karen officials were debating about what to do with us.

I felt that the time had come for me to make an appeal to God to grant us freedom. By now I had become a convinced Catholic, except that I was not yet baptized and formally received into the Church. But I had lost all my Christian fellow-prisoners, the Catholic officer, God's instrument in my conversion, the Anglican, killed by a splinter from the hand grenade, and an elderly Baptist Kareni civilian, shot by the villagers. If I were to face death after this triple tragedy, I would have no Christian friend nearby to give me emergency baptism.

One day about the middle of August I began a novena to the Sacred Heart of Jesus to obtain our freedom. On the afternoon of the sixth day a friendly Karen from the village came to tell us that our own troops were approaching. He and our guards took us to a hillside near the hospital and left us there. In less than half an hour the first of our liberators climbed up the hill shouting our names and calling on the Karens to give us up. We shouted back and then we had a most emotional reunion.

At our request the troops refrained from pouring mortar and machine-gun fire into the village. We found the nurses on the hill, trying to flee. I told them to return to their hospital and also to tell their people who had run away to return to their homes. The troops would behave with kindness and sympathy towards them.

Then we left with our soldiers for Toungoo.

It was a three-day march through the jungle. All along the way I continued my novena prayers. On the ninth and last day of the novena we arrived in Toungoo.

On the night before our arrival we had a most happy reunion. My friends, senior officers and a guerrilla leader, all comrades of the Independence movement, came out to our camp to welcome us. We talked through the night. I told them that I had decided to become a Catholic and would like to devote myself to missionary work. None of them raised any objection. They were all understanding and sympathetic.

On the afternoon of my arrival in Toungoo I sought out the priest who had visited the Catholic officer in prison more than two years earlier. I told him all I knew about our friend's death. Then I asked for baptism.

The priest said that I should first place myself under a spiritual director and study the Catholic doctrine systematically. Then I could decide whether I still wished to be a Catholic.

It was a reasonable proposal. To enable me to carry it out, the Father gave me a letter of introduction to a priest in Rangoon.

About two months after our liberation I was baptized, taking Augustine as my Christian name. No word of objection to my decision or of disapproval was uttered by my father, my sisters, my step-mother, my friends or my superiors.

God had shown me every mercy and granted me a wealth of graces to make me understand His will. Slowly He converted me, making me act and endure according to His design and not according to my own desires. I tried, later, to enter a religious order but in that I failed. That, too, was God's will for me.   But whatever may be the service that He wishes me to render, I await His bidding.

Notes

LIGHT SHONE IN A PRISON

[1] Catholics honor the Sacred Heart of Jesus as the symbol of His divine love.   In devotion to the Sacred Heart they seek to return love for love by showing gratitude, offering reparation for ingratitude and by humble confidence.

[2] The Rosary is a simple system of prayer in which people think of Christ's life, death and resurrection in a series of 15 episodes, which they review in spiritual union with Mary, His mother.   For each episode they recite the Lord's Prayer (the Our Father) and ten Hail Marys as accompaniment to their meditation. The Hail Mary consists of two short parts, the first comprising the salutations addressed to Mary and recorded in St. Luke's Gospel, the second a request for her intercession.   Rosary beads are used to help in following the orderly plan of the prayer through each of three sets of five episodes.   Each set is begun with the Apostles' Creed (I believe in God, the Father Almighty...).

MY SEARCH

by Mary Pan Wei

Mary Pan Wei is the wife of Professor Paul Tsun-shu Wei, Dean of the College of Commerce of National Cheng Chi University, Taiwan. Her account appeared first in the annual of Providence Girls' College of Taichung, Taiwan. The translation from Chinese was made by Eunice Shih, B.A.

I was brought up in a strongly Buddhist family. For generations my mother's people have been very pious Buddhists. In such an environment my mother was reared and trained to be a typically devout Buddhist with a tender and tranquil nature. She cultivated virtue so well that she was able to treat others courteously, sincerely, devotedly and with dignity. She conformed to all the rules of her faith and so developed a spirit of self-sacrifice. Consequently she was known as a truly Buddha-hearted Buddhist laywoman.

We were a very large family. Four generations lived together. Under my mother's influence, my uncles and aunts, brothers and sisters had great faith in Buddha. On the fast days before each Buddhist festival we all, both the elders and the children, joined in doing penance and chanting the liturgy. I still remember how my third aunt, when I was just

132

learning to talk, taught me to say, "Hear me, O Buddha, O Buddha!" At the age of thirteen or fourteen my brother Chan could repeat the "Diamond Sutra."[1]

When she was middle-aged my mother started to keep long fasts. During the Buddhist fast days of February, June and September each year, we lived entirely on a vegetarian diet. A mendicant Buddhist priest and a mendicant nun, who had left their own homes, carried out the ceremony in which my mother made the five vows. She had taken another step in her religion.

In 1923 she was received into a nunnery at Anch'ing.[2] When the leaf was burning over her head during a magnificent ritual, my brother and I were so affected that we knelt down and prayed. After that we determined to keep a regular fast. On every festival we also went to the temple to be present at the ceremony, not only to serve Mother but also to express our own faith.

We were accustomed to read the canons of Buddhism in order to understand the truth. Our friend, Mr. Hu Chia-tai, professor of the department of philosophy of Wu-Han[2] University and Anch'ing University, had made a deep study of Buddhism. We often held discussions with him and we learned the meaning of the Vehicles or Conveyances — Mahayana, Hinayana,[4] etc., the Buddhist sects Ch'an Tsung and Mi Tsung,[5] and the doctrine by which one sees one's own nature by the light of one's intelligence.

Our home town, Anch'ing, on the Wan-shui River, was hilly and had uneven streets. Our house was built on a slope of the hill; on the second floor we had a shrine of Buddha so placed that it stood directly facing the Yingkiangku temple.

During World War II we who were students moved with Wu-Han University in Central China to Chiating in Szechwan, West China. Chiating is near the beautiful, wooded Mount Omi, where many venerable Buddhist priests lived. We often visited the great Buddhist temple and also Wu-yu temple. The religious libraries attached to these possessed many books on Buddhism.

When the Japanese invasion came to Anch'ing, my mother insisted that we should remain where we were studying. In the autumn of 1938 letters from our family ceased to come. We received no news at all. I wandered from room to room in the house where we lived and knew no peace by day or by night.

In the summer of 1939 friends sent me the sad news from my home town of the slaughter and depredation committed by the invading forces. My brother was confronted by disaster and died. Within seven hours of his death my sister-in-law committed suicide. My mother, widowed from her thirty-eighth year, began to live with one of my brothers, her only surviving son. How could she endure such suffering at her advanced age? I learned that she died shortly after the calamity that befell the family. None of my relatives are willing, even now, to tell me of what illness, when or why my mother died.

Did such grievous misfortune ever before exist on the earth? Did anyone suffer more than I during the invasion? Though we may not have sown good seed, we should not have harvested such bad fruit. That was how I felt. As a result, my health broke down and my faith wavered. In the midst of our national adversity, my resentment against the invader and my ill health, I despaired and became a complete atheist.

After the victory in 1945, our people gradually returned to their former condition and took a fresh lease on life. But my heart was in rebellion. I had a strong desire to go back to my home in Anch'ing but I lacked courage to adapt myself to my miserable circumstances. Sorrow and illness were my companions.

On my way home from Chiating to Anch'ing I was hospitalized three times. Consequently I did not arrive back until the winter of 1946.

I found my home wholly changed, after the great chaos. The buildings had fallen, and my relatives had departed from this world, with the exception of one aged cousin and one of my very young relatives. These had experienced so many woes and so much bitterness that they were reluctant to recall any of their heart-breaking ordeals.

The trees in the back yard of our house were withered. Our shrine of the Buddha, our picture of Buddha, our bells, drums, jars and metal rings had all been destroyed during the war. This lovely, quiet place for doing penance and for worshipping Buddha had become miserable. How could I have faith now when everything was lost?

Shortly afterwards the bandits became rampant and powerful. In the spring of 1947 the bandits from Tapieh mountain, on the boundary between Hupeh and Anhui provinces, were overrunning the land. The people living two or three miles from the town were existing from hand to mouth and were in such danger that I dared not go to visit my parents' graves with libations and offerings.

Such difficulties, added to bitterness of heart and bodily infirmity, brought about a psychosomatic condition and resulted in insomnia. Not long after this the Communist forces crossed the river and the

China Mainland changed color. I was forced to flee from Anch'ing to Nanking, then to Shanghai and to Kwangchow, and thence to Taiwan. Unable to find a permanent abode, we had no peace in our lives.

Under the constantly changing conditions I had no time to yield to my worries. Worn out, too, from my long, tiring journeys, I became exhausted. Since I could not sleep, my health did not improve. Friends advised me to look for the true faith with understanding, so that I might once more become the master of my soul.

One day Father Kung was at Mrs. Chen Shih-ch'uan's home, giving instructions. She wanted me to hear him, but at that time I was scarcely able to walk, as my right leg was paralyzed. Mrs. Chen, however, helped me to the place where the instructions were being given.

Father Kung was telling who God is. God is the Creator, he said, and the true Lord of the universe, of angels, of men and of all things; He created everything and He is the Source of sources. He added that God is most merciful, that with joy He forgives all those who are heartily sorry for their sins.

At this time I was suddenly touched. It seemed as though a veil was being lifted, and I prayed silently.

Father Kung sent me a catechism, which I read sometimes in my sickbed. Though I could not understand many things in the book, I longed to know God.

Mrs. Chen went to America, and we moved to a suburb, Peihu. A few months later, my old classmate, Mrs. Wei, introduced me to Father Maurus Fang-hao, from whom I took instructions for six months. He told me that to know the true faith is the most important thing in one's life and that after we believe that there is a true God, we should take a further step and bear witness to His existence. He lent me a copy of the "Explanation of the Catechism," in which we read of things that give witness to the existence of God and the reasons why we believe in Him. How many ideas you can get from this book depends on your understanding and faith.

"You have the true faith now," Father Fang told me. "I wish that your husband could also become interested in eternity and be baptized at the same time as you receive baptism."

At the end of the year we moved to a hostel at Cheng Chi University at Mucha. There we had to endure two severe typhoons and were also frightened by flood. My insomnia, which had made me somewhat hysterical, flared up again, as a result of these perils, and I was hospitalized for four months. I would take four or five sleeping pills, but in vain. Dr. Tang said that I was a kind of hypochondriac and affirmed that my condition could be cured by psychoanalysis later. Twice a week I went back to my home.

One day, seeing my husband in the study, praying before a holy picture, I was so touched that I seemed to have received the light of truth. My peace of mind returned and I became much stronger.

After that, my husband and I began to talk about the cultivation of virtue. He advised me: "Read one chapter of the Gospel each day, and God will give you guidance, instruction and consolation. If our hearts are really resting in God we can be saved. Whenever we do something wrong, we can confess our faults to God. He is almighty and all knowing. He even knows the secrets in the depths of our hearts."

After hearing this, that night, I felt very peaceful and made acts of contrition over and over again.

From that time I understood that this atheist, my husband, was really hoping to become a Catholic. In the meantime Father Mark Tsai often paid us a visit. My husband became more devout day by day. Every Sunday morning before seven o'clock he went to church for Mass. I am sure that God's influence had something to do with that. We often discussed questions of religion. Though I was still suffering from some disquiet of mind, I kept silence whenever prayers were being said.

In April, 1962, I came home from the hospital. Father Mark Tsai began to give us instruction and to discuss problems with us once a week. Through the enlightment he brought, all my troubles disappeared. Gradually I could sleep without any sleeping pills.

On June 2, 1963, my husband and I were baptized. He took the Christian name of Paul; I was christened Mary. Since our baptism we have assisted at Mass at seven o'clock every Sunday morning, regardless of the weather. Consistently we say our morning and night prayers. We have received the sacrament of Confirmation. We feel that our hearts are directed towards God and that from now on we may be leading others to God and still be loving others and all things according to God's holy will.

Notes

MY SEARCH

[1] A sutra is a doctrinal discourse, usually a series of aphorisms.

[2] Often spelled Anking, a city of Anhwei province in East Central China.

[3] Wu Han in Central China is the triple city comprising Hankow, Hanyang and Wuchang.

[4] Mahayana, the Greater Vehicle, differs from the older form of Buddhism, the Theravada system. Mahayana was developed by the Northern Buddhists of India about the beginning of the Christian era. Its followers have given the name Hinayana or Lesser Vehicle, regarded as somewhat derogatory, to Theravada Buddhism, which is found in South-East Asia from Sri Lanka (Ceylon) and Burma to Saigon, where the two systems meet. From Saigon north to China and Japan, Buddhists follow the Mahayana form. There are many different sects within these two broad divisions.

[5] Ch'an Tsung is a meditative school of Buddhism in which instruction is to be oral, not from books. Mi Tsung is a Buddhist sect that prevails in Tibet.

THE NEW VISION

The Story of Choi Nam-Son

by Paul Rhee

This account of the Korean author,
Choi Nam-Son, is translated from an article
by Paul Rhee, published in the monthly
review, *Kyong Hyang* (Seoul), in October,
1970. It marked the thirteenth anniversary of the death of Choi Nam-Son. Paul
Rhee was a disciple of his and served as
secretary to him in his last years. This
translation is included here by permission
of the editor of *Kyong Hyang,* Father
Angelo Kim. The translator is Father
Hugh MacMahon, Columban missionary
in Seoul.

There is much truth in the old Korean saying
that a great tree is buffeted by many winds. Choi
Nam-Son, who had the Buddhist name "Yuk Dang"
and later received the Christian name Peter, can be
numbered among the great men of our time because
of his outstanding achievements, and truly it can be
said of him that he was caught up in many important
happenings.

He was born on April 26, 1890, in Seoul.
During his youth Korea was passing through an
agonizing period of history, emerging out of seclusion

to cope with revolutions within and invasions from without. At the age of fifteen, when his country was plunged in the whirlpool of events at the outbreak of the Russian-Japanese war, he was selected for an imperial scholarship and along with the sons of fifty high government officials he was sent to attend the Chu-I (First) Middle School in Tokyo. However, nothing appealed to his scholarly interest there and, considering it useless to continue studying in a place where he found nothing for him to learn, he soon returned home. Two years later, he went back to Japan and enrolled in the History Department of élite Waseda University Law School. However, even there he was not satisfied. After only two months he decided to return home and brought back with him books on the New (Western) culture along with a printing press.

Since by that time Korea had become a protectorate of Japan, Choi Nam-Son started a new cultural movement and was determined to plan for national independence. It was for that reason that he had acquired the printing press and he intended to use it in the important task of enlightenment. In 1907 he opened the New Gate Institute publishing house. In the following November he published "Youth" magazine, the first mass-circulation magazine in Korea. In this publication he printed "From the Ocean to Youth," which introduced a new type of poetry to journalism.

When Korea was annexed by Japan in 1910, Choi Nam-Son or Yuk Dang, keenly feeling the national humiliation, restarted the Shining Gate Society of Korea. If the New Gate Institute could be said to have national enlightenment as its goal, the Shining Gate Society of Korea sought to preserve the outstanding Korean classics from Japanese destruction.

In 1911 "Youth" magazine was forcibly shut down but Choi Nam-Son refused to yield and successively founded the "Red Jacket," "Ideal Boy" and "New Star" magazines. In 1914 he began to publish the high-class magazine "Clear Spring." He composed the Declaration of Independence, which was to be used in the 1919 March the First Independence Movement, and for this he was given two-and-a-half-years penal servitude.

When he emerged from prison in 1919, he returned to his publications. At the age of 33 he dissolved the New Gate Institute and started the Eastern Brightness Society with a weekly named "Eastern Brightness." Following this in 1924, he brought out a daily newspaper called "The Era Daily Report." However, because of financial difficulties and the opposition of the Japanese authorities, it did not last long.

From 1925 most of his time was taken up with writing books. In 1928 his relationship with the Japanese-formed Editors' Society of Chosen (Korea) caused much public comment from his fellow intellectuals. Even though his strong patriotic sense had never weakened, after Liberation he was accused of being anti-national and was confined in West Gate Prison, Seoul. This was in 1949, when he was sixty years old.

With the North Korean invasion of June 25, 1950, he became a refugee in Pusan, and the many valuable classics which he had gathered with such care were burned in his Seoul house. In Pusan, and later when he returned to Seoul, he devoted all his energies towards helping in the reconstruction of his fatherland and promoting the national consciousness of his countrymen.

The National History of Korea, Korean Common Sense, The Common Sense of 30 Million People,

Korean Culture, and *The History of Overcoming National Crises* were among the books he published. His most ambitious work, however, *A Dictionary of Korean History,* was left unfinished, due to his death from cerebral hemorrhage.

On November 17, 1955, he had been received into the Catholic Church and on October 10, 1957, he died.

Choi Nam-Son was outstanding, not just as one of the pioneers of Korean journalism but also as a conscientious individual. He gave up the Buddhism he had followed for forty years and became a Catholic, His interest in Catholicism began in his youth, when he studied sociology. The more recent history of Korea is bedewed with the blood of Catholic martyrs, Reading the life of some of these heroes, he was greatly impressed. He was not baptized, however, until November, 1955. The event could not go unnoticed. The long article on Life and Religion which he wrote at that time was a proclamation of his conversion. And just as his Proclamation of National Independence ensured his reputation among future generations, his baptismal proclamation is a landmark for posterity, composed by a man who, while showing a deep concern for the future of his country, sought his personal road to salvation.

Rather than trace the events leading to Choi Nam-Son's conversion, as one who was close to him in life and who received and wrote down the original of his proclamation of faith, I will follow that proclamation in which he recorded the thoughts of his heart.

At the outset he states: "The relationship between life and religion is very similar to that between the human body and air, especially in the fact that it cannot leave the element in which it is nourished," thus pointing out the absolute necessity of religion.

"When a person comes to realize that his life is a very frail thing, he feels an unlimited desire for life. When he becomes conscious of the weakness of his ability, he gets a desire for unlimited power. This desire for life and power is man's drive for self-improvement." Thus he compared religious faith with self-improvement.

As to the question, "Which religion is the best?" he states: "Religion is not just the practice of a theory. It has salvation as its goal, and the final judgment to be passed on a religion depends on how it fulfils this purpose." Also: "Although the help provided by religion is basically personal, in certain situations the state of the country, the world and public morals demands that it be applied to the collective needs of the people as a nation." Thus he defined the social aspect of religion and the sense of human solidarity.

He regarded religion as the spiritual basis necessary for Korea's development as a truly democratic nation, "Korea is now liberated politically. Historically it is established as a new nation, and a new culture is being created, but when you view this situation you cannot but notice the lack of a worthwhile spiritual foundation. Rather, there is little change from the situation which existed one or two centuries ago... In the teachings of the Church, which are concerned with the religious aspect of world culture and were revealed through the people of Israel and have been carefully studied and completed, one finds the philosophy of Christ. One also finds in the Church the organizational genius of the Romans and the essence of modern thought.

"While the Catholic principles for the spiritual

life can be expressed almost sufficiently by the Buddhist terms of Vividness, Delicacy, Solemnity, and the Ability to Encourage, with regard to religious truth even the mystical "Ten Dark (Secrets)" of the *Hwa-Om* (Scripture) and the "Three Borders" of the *Pop-Hwa* (i.e. the best doctrines of Buddhism) fall far below Catholicism in expressing the deepest mysteries of universal life."

He adds: "As Creator, Christ stated the first principles of all things on heaven and earth, and by divine power and Providence He explains the order and harmony between things. So with regard to personal salvation and the ability to guide the resurrection of our nation it (the Catholic Church) is lacking in no respect." Thus he reasoned that the Catholic faith was a necessary foundation for the spiritual culture of the nation.

"At this point I felt that I had found in Catholicism what I had sought far and wide from Confucianism, Buddhism and the other religions but could not find. Moreover, when I came to understand the sense of union with God and of escape from the bonds of darkness, as that sense of union and escape was felt by the Sages[1] of over a hundred years ago who introduced Catholicism, my joy was boundless." His happiness on entering the Catholic Church can easily be imagined.

Choi Nam-Son was also enthusiastic about the influence of the Gospel message on the Catholic world and the circumstances by which it came into Korea itself. "In the 16th century the Jesuits entered Peking and put into practice the command of Jesus that his gospel be preached everywhere. But Korea, the 'forbidden country of the Orient,' did not wait for missionaries to come, it brought in the message by the efforts of its own people. Such a case is unprecedented in the spread of religious ideas and clearly shows the Providence of God. In the world there are many religions, and from the beginning of the world right up to now, there have been many conversions from one faith to another. However, few have had a continuous unifying effect, intellectually and culturally, and a consistency in activity. The Catholic Church has shown a changeless and unique ability to nurture world thought in a positive way and protect it."

Then, having given a historical outline of the effect of Catholicism on world thought and specified that in the Catholic Church the true gospel of personal salvation and human improvement is to be found, he goes on to say: "By all means discuss Korean social progress, but first, if you want to find a spiritual foundation, give careful and fair attention to the Catholic Church. That Church is not a recently appeared castle-in-the-air but an edifice founded on rock which does not shake in the wind and which has been tested by a long history of events."

He adds: "Right now the future of Korea must be confided to trustworthy safeguards, that is, it must be safeguarded by the Catholic faith."

Finally, giving heartfelt thanks to God, Choi Nam-Son had this to say of his own conviction: "On the 7th of November, 1955, I liquidated the religious bonds of fifty to sixty years. I turned to the Catholic faith and by receiving baptism, I sought not only my personal salvation but also the answer to the deep desires of our present generation for a new national vision and sought also to complete the task left unfinished by the Sages of two hundred years ago. I hope that this outline will contribute to the worldwide search for what is right. It is with thanks to God for the immeasurable grace of this vision which He has opened to me that I write these words."

Note

THE NEW VISION

[1] These are the Korean scholars who, around the year 1777, obtained books of Catholic doctrine while on the annual official visit to Peking. Together they studied these books, written by Jesuit missionaries in China, and decided that Christianity is the true religion. One of them was baptized in Peking in 1783. Others followed his example. They shared their knowledge of Christianity with other Koreans, so that when the first priest came to Korea in 1794, the Chinese Father James Chu, there were already about 4,000 Christians in the country. Thus Christianity was introduced and implanted in Korea by lay Korean apostles.

MY JOURNEY

by Father Thomas M. Bu'u Du'o'ng, O.P.

The writer of this account, professor of philosophy in the University of Saigon, is a descendant of the Emperors Minh Mang and Tu Duc under whom Vietnamese Christians suffered severe persecution during the nineteenth century. He is now a priest of the Order of Preachers — the Dominicans — and is superior of his vice-province and president of the Union of Major Superiors of Religious Orders in Vietnam. The following is part of a travel journal, written by him on board the *André Lebon* en route to France, in 1935, seven years after he became a Catholic and five years before he was ordained a priest. He was traveling to France to study and prepare for the priesthood.

On the morning of October 24 (1935) I left Hue. The first stage of my journey would be to Nha Trang, to pay my respects to my father, who was stationed there as Chief of Province.

Usually the train from Hanoi arrived in good time, but this day it was an hour late. I had set out for the station very early and now I had to wait. At the station it was still dark and the wind had risen. The cold of the morning mist was felt by myself and my relatives who had come with me.

148

Today, recalling their great kindness, I ask God to bless all who, in the charity of their hearts, help those who have dedicated themselves to His service.

I had often made this journey, but by car, in my younger days when the world smiled on me and earthly renown was my goal. Now, traveling by the railway, I crossed the plains and wound my way around mountains with a light heart. The pursuit of renown has yielded to the pursuit of virtue, Formerly, loving this life, I devoted myself to it; today, while still loving it, I want to bring it into harmony with truth.

So, formerly and recently, making the same journey, seeing the same landscape with the mountains and rivers, chatting with the other travelers, I am the same person, but now how much changed! Realizing the happiness that is now mine, thinking of the happiness to which I aspire, I regret the twenty years of my youth. when I was carried away by the current of error and disorder. How can I recover them? Are young people going through these years always making mistakes as I did? After straying for a certain time, do they listen to the voice of the Spirit warning them?

Thanking God for having taken pity on me, I pray to Him for others.

By chance, during this train journey, I met Uncle S. He is a very intelligent man, gifted with all the talents. He can play the guitar, play chess, write poetry and paint (the four accomplishments of the old-time *literati*). He also has wasted his youth. The efforts he made in his studies under the Brothers had enabled him only to enter the higher school of public works, and obtain the diploma of *agent technique*. After his crises, his faith, or lack of it, remains unchanged — a "faith" without worship of God or belief in Buddha.

Still, however, he holds the Catholic religion in high esteem. He remembers the Catholic doctrine he learned during religion classes taught by the Brothers. Frequently he admits that it is true. But why has he not got the faith yet? Is it perhaps because he has not received the grace? Or is he still so strongly attached to the things of this world that he cannot hear the voice of God? I do not venture to guess. It is a personal question between God and him. Only God and my uncle know the answer.

There is nothing unique in the state of this soul. One could say that my Uncle S. represents a great number of the youth of Vietnam. Personally I rank him among my benefactors who have helped me on the road from Buddhism to Christianity. If he hears this, he is sure to be surprised. But, Uncle dear, I beg you not to jump to the conclusion that you have been able to convert a soul. Rather, thank God for having deigned to make use of you in matters you did not think about and to which you gave no heed.

My meeting with Uncle S. on the train led me to look back over my spiritual journey.

Formerly I was very hostile to Christianity, to such a point that I did not want to have anything whatever to do with priests or lay Christians. I had never read a book dealing with Christianity. I went to such an absurd extreme that on seeing the word "God" I was displeased and used only the word "Heaven." I forbade the use of the word "God" in classes given to little children. Truly this antipathy was bringing me to the stage of folly.

Forgive me, Lord, this extraordinary repugnance! You know how my heart, in all sincerity, went astray, following preconceived ideas, and then transgressed. . . .

During the year when I had to prepare for the

final examination of my secondary studies, Uncle S.
was staying with us. Although we were not attending the same school, we were in the same year and
were preparing for the same examination, he in the
school of the Christian Brothers and I in the govern-
ment-run *lycée*. Consequently we had much in
common to talk about. We were always in accord
on subjects concerning our studies and amusements,
but whenever we incautiously raised the question of
faith and religion, we could not keep from arguing.
"Arguing" is too strong a word, perhaps, for although I took the offensive in strong terms, through
hostility, Uncle S. was not defending a faith held by
himself. Hence in spite of the heat on the attack-
ing side, the defense remained always moderate and
conciliatory, never becoming partisan, simply repeating the truths heard from the Brothers.

Rare were these occasions when we talked about
religion. That is not surprising. Since we were
living in a pagan atmosphere, all questions of faith
and religion were matters that had no importance
for us and we did not waste time in discussing them.

However rare these occasions were, it was
during them that one or two conversations made an
impression on my soul. Today I can still recall one
of them. It was late at night and we were sitting,
in the cool air, under the moonlight, in front of the
house on the river bank. We were talking about
subjects of no great interest. Like all young folk,
we let our conversation range over everything, except questions of religion and virtue. Then, I am
not sure why, we brought up the subject of religion.
It seems to me that it was in connection with a for-
tune-teller, a soothsayer, whom we had consulted
about the result of our forthcoming examination.
Perhaps in referring to this incident, we had spoken
of faith and religion.

I opened up the discussion as follows:

"Buddhism is very interesting," I said, "but Buddha is not the Creator. So we believe that Heaven has created us and looks after us and yet we have never worshipped Heaven. We only make offerings to Buddha and we behave any way we like. We also worship Confucius and believe in fortune-tellers. Man is indeed a strange being."

Immediately Uncle S. said: "The Christians are not at all like that. They believe in God, Who is Providence, the Creator. They do not worship and believe unreasonably, as we do. Likewise the Jews, but these are still awaiting the coming of the Saviour, while the Christians believe that Jesus is the Saviour. Interpreting the Old Testament in their own way, the Jews do not want to believe in Jesus. . . ."

In actual fact, centuries before Jesus Christ was born, the prophets in the Old Testament foretold the time and place of His birth, His life in poverty and His painful, dramatic death. The Jews still believe in these prophecies but they do not wish to believe in Jesus. . .

This is the evidence that has struck me most forcibly. Thus my uncle and others like him, such as Doctor D. and Engineer C., former classmates, all pagans, without realizing or paying attention, played an important part in the process of my conversion to Catholicism. Perhaps God has been too indulgent to me since, knowing that my antipathy kept me from consorting with Christians and from asking them questions, He made use of pagans to arouse my soul.

The words spoken by others, though they made me reflect, were not strong enough to break down the barriers that separated me from Christianity.

God allowed me to discover the truthfulness and the wonders of religion in books. The words of Uncle S. had indeed impressed me, but at that time of preparation for examinations all other matters were set aside — and more especially the question of religion for a young pagan lad. Consequently I continued calmly to venerate Buddha and to hate Christianity.

The day I passed my examination I went for a walk. I entered the Dac-lap bookshop and bought some books. Now that I had reached my longed-for goal, I indulged my fancy by buying some unseemly volumes. Ashamed of myself, however, for having bought books of that kind, I took two others, *Le Génie du Christianisme* by Chateaubriand and the *Pensées* of Pascal. It really was not for reading that I bought them, for I knew well that these are books written in praise of Christianity. While I liked the style of Chateaubriand and that of Pascal, I was no reader of books that spoke well of Christianism.

These innocuous books had to suffer the fate of remaining undisturbed in a corner until the day when I was arranging my belongings before leaving for Hanoi to prepare to enter the university. Before packing them in a trunk to leave them at home, I happened to open the *Pensées*. I came upon a page on which I read some lines. I found them interesting and full of meaning. At the same time it seemed that something of extraordinary force took hold of me in my very soul. I decided then to bring the two books with me.

More than once I found that many passages in these works left me puzzled. In reality they only made me sympathetic to Christianity but not yet convinced.

It was only after having acquired this sympathy that I set myself to study the matter. Many a time my soul could not find peace. It seemed that I had to go through a terrible struggle, and that lasted for three full years.

I still remember those times in college, during the hours of recreation when I did not join in any game, or in the late hours of the night, when I could not sleep, or at home in the evening, when I was alone after having played some melodies that I had just learned, or having made some drawings. At these times I began to reflect and ask myself: "Christianity is right — should I yield my assent to it?"

Ought I to embrace it? That is unreasonable! Never! Never! It is right and correct — that is true. But "I will go home and bathe in my own pond. Whether the water is clear or murky, a pond of one's own is always better." Truly my obstinacy was making me foolish. This proverb is only the saying of a proud and wayward man. Applied to religion, in particular, it makes no sense.

While still considering the Christian religion as a foreign creed, I did not advert to the fact that Sakya Mouni (Buddha) was a Hindu, Confucius was Chinese and that Jesus was not a European, but He is adored throughout Europe solely because Christians believe that He is God and they adore God alone.

God is common to all the peoples of the world and is not special for this or that individual country. When He came into this world, He was born in the midst of the Israelite people. Unquestionably this people could then be called unique in the world, for they adored God alone and had not fallen into the error of the pantheist doctrine found in India and China or into the pitfall of polytheism like Greece and Rome, though these were civilized countries at that period.

Amid other peoples, the Jewish people remain still faithful to the Creator, although they cannot escape having some members imbued with morals of the East or of the West. But they are unanimous regarding their obligation to worship God. Perhaps this is why God has chosen this people. Assuredly there are many other mysteries that I cannot wholly penetrate.

So Christ is God for all. Everybody then is bound to adore Him, to love Him, to serve Him, to obey His Commandments and to keep His word.

As regards eminent men, any person living in any country can take the trouble to reflect on a subject and teach others, believing that this is useful for human society. Such a person hopes to bring happiness to mankind. In spite of his failings or mistakes, we ought to respect what is good and disregard what is bad, accept what is reasonable and reject the false theories, avoiding both obstinacy and contempt. The human mind, enjoying neither the grace of direct revelation nor the light of the Church's teaching, but relying only on its unaided reasoning, wishes to reflect on the mysteries of the universe and to inquire into questions of life and death. How could it avoid falling into many errors?

Let us not speak of those who are in error through pride and who refuse to change, holding stubbornly to false doctrine and thus doing harm to human souls. But I speak of the sages and philosophers or the bonzes who lived in a period or a situation in which they could not hear about the true religion. How, then, could they escape error in their belief? Realizing that, we cannot blame them but we must respect them. They are heroic figures, full of virtues and talents in philosophy and religion. What is indispensable is to remain in accord with the natural law. But we must not transgress the limits of veneration by transforming our respect into a cult or form of worship, treating these sages and heroes as supernatural spirits, of the same rank as the Creator of the universe.

What is the order, the hierarchy of beings? How must we distinguish the Most High from mere man, the Creator from his creatures?

Even the renowned wise men, like Socrates, Plato and Aristotle of Greece, Confucius of China or the celebrated monks who became Buddhas in India, all declared that they were men who had studied to acquire knowledge and had practised virtue in order to arrive at what they became. Even Confucius said: "I was not born with infused knowledge. Like the holy man and the wise man, I have commenced by perceiving, studying incessantly, correcting people unwearyingly, and that is all I can say."

Sakya Mouni himself, even though he took the title of Buddha, said: "Every man has within him the capacity to become a Buddha." Therefore anybody can become a Buddha on condition that he takes the trouble of applying himself to the elimination, in all sincerity, of his personal desires and of withdrawing himself from the world. Thus a day will come when one becomes clear-minded and free or, in other words, "enlightened," that is to say, a Buddha. Buddhas, therefore, are men who have detached themselves from the world and devoted themselves untiringly to the practice of perfection. They are not gods.

To these persons we owe respect, while our adoration is due to God alone, who has created us and protects us. If we do not know His religion and His teachings, we should investigate, study and reflect, in order to know. If we remain indifferent, we are like children who do not wish to know their own parents. Such an attitude cannot fail to imply sinning against filial piety and the duty of gratitude.

It is only in recent years that I have been thinking along these lines. Formerly, unfounded hostility and unreasonable prejudices blinded my mind, which, determined never to yield assent to Christianity, was absolutely unwilling to reflect. This went so far as to try to stifle the inner voice that never ceased calling on me to study the question of truth in depth.

Who, then, is he who writes these lines? I have to smile on thinking about it. . . . Truly, my God, You love me too much, for I have been so unruly. You continue to make use of all means to bring me back to You. Your only desire is that I should enjoy true happiness and escape eternal suffering. . . .

More and more I was convinced of the truth of Catholicism, but I could not think of being baptized. I put this issue aside every time it came to my mind. Many of the things I saw in my Catholic compatriots seemed to me to be too foreign to our culture and customs: their more or less Frenchified life and way of speaking, their churches and ceremonies that seemed more European than of universal character. For me, loving the Confucian culture as I did and respecting the austere life of the Buddhist monks, there was still another obstacle to conversion to Catholicism. It was the life led by many Catholics and by some of their priests, a life that seemed to me to be too free. I could not regard them as believers and servants of God.

One day, while attending my grandfather, who was receiving a visit from a Buddhist mandarin, I heard the latter speak in praise of an abbey of Cistercians that a missionary had recently founded near Hue. The life of these monks impressed me deeply.

My knowledge of their way of living and my admiration for it finished by convincing me and making me decide to become a Christian. Accordingly I applied to the Prior of this abbey and received baptism from his hands on August 15, 1928.

THE PATH ILLUMINED BY MUTUAL UNDERSTANDING

by Ananda

"Ananda" was a Buddhist monk in Sri Lanka (Ceylon) up to 1966. While still a monk, he entered the university for higher studies. He had already met a Catholic priest, a contact that aroused his interest in Christianity. Concurrently with his university studies he learned more about the Christian religion and found in it fulfilment of his spiritual aspirations. In his quest he realised that mutual understanding between Buddhists and Christians removes obstacles to true enlightenment.

Six years ago I took a momentous step. I took it neither hastily nor without due reflection. I had in fact been considering it for nearly eleven years. It was momentous to me, because it represented the most significant decision of my life and also because it seemed unexpected in the light of my background, traditions and training.

Until I took that step when I was 36, I belonged to the prominently respectable majority in my country — namely the Sinhala Buddhists. And being a member of the *Sangha* (the Buddhist clergy), that is a monk, I was literally "worshipped" by the Buddhist devotees living around the temple.

But I was not happy about the entire set-up in the monastic life. I felt that I was a prisoner in a bleak narrow cell. Hence to keep myself from yielding to despair, I thought of continuing my secular studies.

At the time my mind was constantly in search of liberation. Of course, it was an enlightened liberation that I was looking for. I did not want just to run away from the temple. In fact, I had great respect for the *Dhamma* (the Buddhist teachings) as expounded by Lord Buddha, but it did not show me the way to true happiness. I realised that true happiness positively existed and was surely attainable with conscious and determined effort. Hence neither annihilation as an ultimate goal, nor cessation of all desires as a means to it, satisfied my aspirations.

It was providential that in 1961 I met a Catholic priest. But it was not his priestly garb that impressed me; rather it was his extraordinary humanity and consideration for others that attracted me. I seized that opportunity to acquaint myself with this man who appeared to have found the secret of happiness in a positive manner.

My new-found friend was very well acquainted with the tenets of Buddhism. On the contrary, my knowledge of Christianity was almost nil. The only Christianity I knew was based on those teachings of the Catholic Church interpreted, or sometimes misinterpreted and misrepresented, by Buddhist critics. I soon realised that they were biased.

But still I hesitated to find out the real truth about Christianity, because I myself was personally not impressed by the Western appearance of the Christian churches and the Western life-styles of their ministers. I felt that a religion which fails to integrate itself into the culture of a people cannot contain the Truth for that people, nor could it lead to the happiness for which I was searching.

However, I took the opportunity of my acquaintance and later friendship with Father X to test some of those accusations made against Catholic clergy in particular. One such accusation was that they are like empty-stomached fishermen, all out to catch whatever fish they could with ever-enticing bait. But I soon realised that I was mistaken, for my friend showed no sign of any interest in influencing me about his religion.

On the contrary, to my amazement, this priest showed a keen interest in the actual practice of temple-life. He told me that he accepted fully certain principles of Buddhism. There were days when he used the *Dhammapada* for his meditation. He was a strong adherent of *ahimsa* (non-violence) towards all creatures.

Once I knew him well, I told him all I had heard about Christianity. He, in his unobtrusive gentle manner, did not try to defend his religion with all sorts of arguments, as I expected him to do. On the contrary, he said he would not blame those who criticized the Church. There were so many blunders inside the Church of God that if it were not for her divine origin she would have faltered in her religious teachings and died a natural death.

While using the weakness of the Church, or rather its human members, as an argument for the ever-present divine element in it, he admitted the fact that due to the use of methods which at that time were common but in the final analysis were psychologically unsound, the "conquistadors" (colonial military conquerors) had impeded the work of the Portuguese missionaries in making Christianity a more flourishing Faith in Sri Lanka. It was natural, he said, that

outsiders judged a religion by the way in which the
adherents of that religion lived.

I was able to appreciate this approach, for I
found almost the same sort of problem existing among
the *Sangha*. For example, the *Dhamma* is dead
against caste, yet caste differences are observed and
even emphasized at the various levels of the *Sangha*.

My priest-friend not only dispelled my wrong
impressions of Christianity but gradually enabled me
to have a better understanding of the Christian teaching and way of life. He didn't preach, but his life
spoke. He showed a genuine desire for the monastic
life.

Father X told me that the Church in Sri Lanka
is in need of a religious order founded on the lines
of Buddhist monastic life. Thus he wanted to in-
carnate Christianity into the local setting so that the
Gospel of Christ would be more meaningful and
understandable to a people who are strongly religious-
minded and have high moral values. I am now convinced that this should be recognized as one important
means of being witnesses of Christ to our Buddhist
brethren.

When on occasions I enquired about the secret
of his abounding happiness, he explained that it was
due to the grace of God. He realised that I understood neither "grace" nor "God." So he added
quickly: "To understand such spiritual things it is
essential that one should experience them."

"To experience and see the truth of a thing"
is something which had much meaning for one. After
all, I followed this exhortation of the Buddha from
my young days. But now that self-same exhortation
turned out to be the turning-point in my attitude
towards Christianity.

As a result of this discussion, my friend offered
me a copy of *Kristu Anusaraya,* the Sinhala version

of *The Imitation of Christ* by Thomas à Kempis. I read it carefully and realised that it carried me a step further than I had reached in all those long years of *bhavana* (meditation) in the temple. The notion of sacrifice was brought out by the author with a higher perspective. With constant reference to the New Testament, he emphasized that it is motivation of the love of God which ennobles sacrifice.

Gradually I realised that the Christian concept of God is supreme in all respects in a positive existence. And I understood that the highest human quality of love was only a glimpse in the manifestation of divine Love, because He is the Creator. Thus a Christian sacrifices something not for mere self-redemption but for the love of a Beloved. This idea gladdened my sorrowful heart. This gladness of heart, I thought, was a grace . . . yes, the grace of God.

Then my friend introduced me to the New Testament. I found Christ full of humanity in spite of His claims to divine power. His lovable humanity and His promise of the life-to-come as everlasting happiness in a real positive way consoled my sickened heart. I realised that my understanding of Christ was becoming clearer with some inner enlightenment.

I was then introduced to the Old Testament. But only a few books of the Old Testament were available in Sinhala. The others were in the process of being translated. My knowledge of English was then not sufficient to understand the English Bible.

In studying English I came across authors full of Christian ideas. Even some poems I learned contained Christian concepts such as the Trinity, Incarnation of the Son of God, Mother of God, Heaven and Hell. Initially, some of them were too disturbing for me. In all such difficulties my friend's

explanations helped me. But his presentation of
some of them as "mysteries" was indeed a stumbling
block on my "Road to Damascus."[1] At this stage
Newman's "Lead, Kindly Light" helped me considerably.[2]

A Buddhist mind abhors mysteries. Further,
the Sinhala word for mystery is "*abirahasa.*" This
doesn't give the correct idea of mystery as in Christianity. It gives an impression of some top-level
secrecy.

However, by lucid explanations my friend succeeded in helping me to get over this difficulty. He
pointed out to me that man himself remains a mystery
in the face of the scientific and technological developments witnessed recently. If that is the case with
the physical phenomena, then, no doubt, those of the
spiritual surpass human intelligence.

Thus I was led to understand the Christian
Faith. I found that it is not something which requires a blind faith, but rather is basically quite
rational. Moreover, it also fits in satisfactorily with
the concept of the nature of the human being. This
perception eventually helped me to realise the relationship with the human nature of the divine Saviour.

In my gradual understanding of the Christian
message, what appealed to me most was Christian
concern for others—for the sick, the destitute, the
sinners. I decided to follow Christ in keeping His
precept of loving one's neighbours as oneself.

Before long I noticed a big change in myself.
My "prison-walls" started to break down; I began
to breathe a new air of freedom. I saw a distant
star waiting to lead my way to everlasting happiness.
I used the New Testament and *The Imitation of
Christ* for my daily meditation more frequently.

In 1963 I got through my University entrance
examination and entered the 'Varsity. By now I

was more proficient in English. This helped me to read the whole Bible and a good deal of Christian literature.

A valuable book that came my way during this period was *The Documents of the Vatican II*. It was only then that I realised how religion should keep in touch with the times, if it is to be relevant, especially to those of the younger generation.

Preoccupation with secular studies did not weaken my search for the truth of Christianity. Meanwhile I made very good progress in my studies and won encomiums from my lecturers. I attributed all these to my better appreciation of the fact that life was worth living, especially when a life of service based on sacrifice and noble ideals was my goal.

I graduated. I had no idea of going back to my temple. But it was not for a Government or private-sector job that I came out of the 'Varsity as a layman. It was to acknowledge Christ as my Master and Lord, Who saved me from the grip of frustration and showed me the path to salvation, happiness and joy, that I put aside the temple robe . . . notwithstanding the fact that I knew very well that I would face the terrifying spectre of unemployment.

There are, I imagine, in all conversions to Christianity phases too personal and intimate to express in words. I cannot write about the final stage, in my own case, more than to say that at that point the problem I had long experienced of having to wait gave way to a firm conviction that I must not wait any longer. Yet even then I felt it must depend upon God's will. By now I was fully instructed about the Christian doctrine and the Catholic way of life.

A very useful consequence is finding peace in religious faith. That certainly I found when I was received into the Church. If I were to sum up in one word what seems to me the most essential gift which becoming a member of the Catholic Church has given to me, I'd say, "Life." I mean a new life, inspired and guided by supernatural grace.

But that is not the end of my personal Odyssey. It was rather a turning point in my spiritual life as a child of God at the age of 36.

It all began, I consider, when my parents took me to the temple when I was just six years old and dedicated me to the Buddhist monastic life, because my horoscope predicted that I would eventually become a chief monk. In retrospect I must admit that although, as a young lad and an adolescent, already garbed in the saffron robe, I went through many a dismal and gloomy spell, still I consider that my path of preparation to find Christ began with that boyhood monasticism. Further, it is unlikely that I would have achieved the enriching friendship with Father X, had I been in another state of life.

On writing to my aging parents, who live with my elder sister 150 miles away from my residence, about my discarding of the robe and my conversion to Christianity, the reply I received was, "Well, *putha* (son), that is your fate!" I hastened to write to them how I interpreted the process as "Providential." And out of consideration for sincere opinion, I added:

> "Call it Fate or Providence, my dearest father and mother, I wish to tell you how true is our Sinhala saying that a life without a friend is a death without a witness. And it was my priest-friend who showed me the way from uncertainty to certainty. Now I possess a new life-giving light. I shall never forget him, just as I shall never forget you, my dearest father and mother."

Notes

THE PATH ILLUMINED BY MUTUAL UNDERSTANDING

[1] It was on the road to Damascus that St. Paul, until then a bitter persecutor of Christians, encountered Christ. From that moment of overwhelming enlightenment he became an ardent follower and apostle of Christ.

[2] A 3-stanza poem written by John Henry Newman while he was still an Anglican, dissatisfied and earnestly seeking the fullness of Christian life and truth. He wrote the poem at sea, in the Mediterranean, on June 16, 1833. In the ensuing years he drew steadily nearer to the Catholic Church and on October 9, 1845 he became a Catholic. Later he became a priest and in 1879 was named a cardinal. A man of great intellect and learning, Newman was one of the most notable converts to the Catholic Church in the century. The second stanza of "Lead, Kindly Light," now a well-known hymn, runs thus:

> *Lead, kindly Light, amid the encircling gloom,*
> *Lead Thou me on!*
>
> *The night is dark, and I am far from home —*
> *Lead Thou me on!*
>
> *Keep Thou my feet; I do not ask to see*
>
> *The distant scene, — one step enough for me.*

THE BELLS OF NAGASAKI KEEP RINGING

by Father Luke H. Inoue

Father Inoue studied in Japan and in the United States. After his return from abroad, he was appointed professor in Eichi University in Amagasaki, in the Archdiocese of Osaka, to which he belongs.

He says that he prefers "to stress the beauty of the Catholic religion" rather than condemn other doctrines. "I believe that many Buddhists would be impressed by the teachings of Jesus Christ, if they were presented in such a manner as to inspire their minds and hearts, without condemning other religions," he writes. It was the positive appeal of Christ's teachings that made him decide to become a Catholic.

On the day of my ordination as priest, I gave to my friends, along with my first priestly blessings, holy cards of the Blessed Virgin Mary with this passage quoted from the Book of Psalms: "How shall I make a return to the Lord for all the good He has done for me?" These are the words that most fittingly expressed my real feeling on that occasion.

This same passage comes back to mind now as I calmly reflect over the years that have passed since that day when I was first received into the Catholic

Church. I find it equally fitting to feel, as did St. John the Apostle, that it was not I who first loved God, but rather it was God who first loved me. Indeed, while as a non-Christian I was walking in the valley of darkness without knowing the true God, I cannot help but feel that it was God who loved me and had plans for me to serve Him at His banquet table. "The favors of the Lord I will sing forever; through all generations my mouth shall proclaim your faithfulness" (Ps. 88:1).

I was born in Osaka, Japan, on January 24, 1935. My family were Buddhists. As a little boy who was amazed at every discovery in the small world around me, I saw grandparents and parents sitting piously every day before the home altar with heads bowed in deep prayer. This little boy felt, saw, and witnessed their happy smile and warm affection as well as their hard work and sacrifices. Indeed, not a moment in the day passed but we children were in the uppermost thoughts of our parents.

As a businessman, my father worked outside all day long. As soon as one of us children heard him opening the door every evening, he would shout, "Dad is back," and we all rushed to him, saying, "Welcome back, Dad! What do you have for us tonight?"

The happiness and joy of my childhood was, however, miserably taken away when the war started. I can hardly forget those dark nights when we spent hours in the underground tunnel while the city was being bombed. Father was outside, always ready to rescue in case the house was destroyed. Mother was with us, saying prayers and clasping my little sister in her arms. I cannot imagine how heart-breaking it was for them to see their children taken away from them and sent to the camp in the less dangerous rural area. While we were away from home, a bomb was dropped right in front of our house, but fortunately it did not explode, and my parents' lives were spared. When the terrible war was finally terminated, the city was found completely destroyed.

It is not easy to describe all the suffering and tribulation that my parents had to go through to raise us in those days. One of their concerns was to find a high school for me to go to. Many school buildings had been destroyed during the war, and many more years were estimated before public schools could be reconstructed. This made them look to private schools, reconstructed to some degree by the help of individuals or a group of people.

One evening, Father came home after having spent a whole day in looking for a school. "I walked," said Father, "for hours and hours in the city. I visited three schools. The last one impressed me the most. The lady secretary treated me cordially." How could he know at that time that it was God who was directing his step and leading him to make a decision?

The school he happened to visit was a Catholic institution run by the Marianist Brothers. Half of the school buildings had been bombed, but the plan for reconstruction was being worked out steadily. "It is a Christian school," said Father, "but I would say that this is the only decent place in the city you could go to at present."

On March 17, 1947, the entrance examination was held, and as Father was taking me to school, a mixed feeling of hope and anxiety filled my mind. When the instructor came to get all the applicants together, Father said in an encouraging tone of voice: "Be confident. You will do well."

The results of this test were posted in a few

days, and how happy my mother and I were to find my name on the list as one of the 240 students accepted to Mei Sei High School, out of over 500 applicants! How proud I was when I was congratulated by my parents, relatives, and grade-school teachers!

At Mei Sei a new life started. Brother Kosugi was in charge of the group in which I was placed. At the first meeting I sensed with a child's perception something different in this man. I found in him a spirit of dedication and sincerity. I immediately felt that I could get along with him easily, and my judgment proved true.

Shortly after I was enrolled, Brother Maeda took us to the chapel. This was, indeed, the first opportunity in my life to visit the House of God. I was struck with the beauty of the altar, the marvelous statue of the Blessed Virgin Mary, and the colourful stained-glass windows. Everything around us made me realize that I was in a solemn place.

Brother gave us a brief explanation of the chapel. When he said, "On that altar there is God," I felt like asking him, "why can I not see God, if He is really present there?" Then I said to myself, "It could be that the spirit of God dwells there." For the first time in my life I learned that Christ was God and He was born of a holy mother named Mary.

In the curriculum table I found a course quite unfamiliar to me. It was a religion class, and I was curious to know what they were going to teach us. Brother Satowaki came to the classroom with a novel in his hand. He said that he was going to read a story for us, and when he finished it, he would ask us how we enjoyed it. The story interested me so much that even today I can recall it in essence. It goes something like this: a knight in a certain country in Europe had a misfortune. Innocent as he was, he saw his father killed. Deprived of his personal property, he was thrown out of his land. He subsequently escaped. While fleeing, he met a monk by the road and told him everything that had happened to him. Although the monk sympathized with him, he could not persuade him to abandon his plans to take revenge on his enemy.

Around that time the bell rang, and the Brother told us to write down at home how we would react to the story. I thought and thought over the story, and imagined what I would have done if I had been the knight. Finally, I wrote that the knight should have had the fortitude to stand up for his deceased father and seek revenge against his enemy. Traditionally, this has been the philosophy of the Japanese warriors, or *samurai,* and I expected my answer to be accepted without question.

At the following religion class, however, I was amazed rather than disappointed to learn of an entirely different point of view. To my surprise, I was told that to forgive was divine and that an act of forgiveness was a virtue. I also learned that Christianity was a religion of forgiveness, and that Jesus Christ died on the Cross to forgive our sins.

Brother Satowaki then read from the Scripture the words of God: "Blessed are they who hunger and thirst for justice, for they shall be satisfied. Blessed are the merciful, for they shall obtain mercy. Blessed are the peacemakers, for they shall be called children of God. Blessed are they who suffer persecution for justice sake, for theirs is the kingdom of heaven. Blessed are you when men reproach you, and persecute you, and speaking falsely, say all manner of evil against you for My sake. Rejoice and exult, because your reward is great in heaven."

The words of God struck me. How beautiful

is the teaching of Jesus Christ!   How noble in reason and how infinite in value!   This concept was entirely different from the teachings of other religions with which I had been acquainted.   I felt a sincere desire to learn more about the teaching of Christ.   I knew that at this moment the grace of God was poured forth upon me urging me to seek and love truth.

I was invited to Sunday Mass in the chapel. While the Mass was celebrated at the altar, Brother Kosugi was leading prayers from the Japanese prayer-book.   The Latin of the Mass did not bother me, although I did not understand it, because I was accustomed to the Buddhist ceremony in which prayers were said by the priests in a strange language. While the Buddhist ceremony seemed to bring forth a solemn, yet a sort of sad, feeling over the deceased, the Catholic Mass appeared to be much more lively and meaningful.   I saw pious men and women at the Mass praying fervently and coming out of the chapel with joy and peace on their faces.   At that time I experienced entirely the same feeling as my sister who said to me when she first came to the church ten years later: "The old people go to the temple, but the young go to Mass."

Brother Kosugi gave me a card with a beautiful prayer, the Our Father, on one side.   One Sunday morning after the Mass he took us to a classroom and explained to us the meaning of the prayer, sentence by sentence.   I loved the prayer and recited it aloud at home, and every time I recited it, I felt better.   I came to see a tremendous difference in content between the Our Father and pagan prayers. While the latter started with petitions with a self-centered motive, the former starts with the praise of God our Father in heaven.   Who could express man's strong urge to adore God in such a simple form as this?   Since I was a child I prayed and loved to pray, but I had never prayed in such a manner, because no one could teach me to pray like this.

In the meanwhile, I felt a voice within me whispering to me that I should become a Catholic. However, as soon as I heard the voice, I hesitated to go further. I was not willing to give up my deep attachment to the home altar that I had cherished for years. One day I asked my parents for permission to become a Catholic, but before I finished speaking, I heard a big "No" from their lips.

"We have our own religion at home. Why do you have to buy a religion from a foreign country?" This was their statement. Indeed, my ancestors have gone into Heaven as good Buddhists, and it is our duty, as I was taught, to please their souls at the home altar every day. The veneration of ancestors is not an essential part of Buddhism but is rather the traditional cult of ancestor worship practised throughout Japan and other Oriental countries. I did not understand yet that it could be done by Catholics as a sign of respect though not as actual religious worship.

I was struck by the beauty of the Catholic religion, but I hated to be unfaithful to the spirit of the family. I was told to wait, and for the following five years I lived a life of spiritual dilemma, walking between the Catholic Church and the Buddhist temple.

One Sunday morning my classmate and I went to visit Brother Satowaki. I wanted to harmonize both my parents' viewpoint and the Catholic one. I asked Brother, "Is it possible to be a Catholic and at the same time to worship at the home altar?"

This would seem too simple a question to ask, but at that time it was a serious matter to me. Brother Satowaki explained to me how contradictory it would be to worship in two ways when we know that there is only one God. I also explained to him about the difficulties in giving up Buddhism and accepting Catholicism. The best solution we reached in our discussion was simply to wait. In the meanwhile, I was encouraged to continue attending Sunday Mass. Fortunately, my parents had no objection to this, because they thought that if the school could offer something worthwhile even on Sunday, they, too, thought it worthwhile to have me in the school. Therefore, by my attending Mass on Sundays they thought they could at least get their money's worth for the tuition they were paying. Moreover, they were confident that as long as I was with my good Christian teachers, I was keeping out of mischief.

In the fall of 1947, we were invited to the theatre to see the film on the twenty-six Japanese martyrs. The movie vividly described the bloody persecution that the Catholics went through in the days of Hideyoshi. Twenty-six men who believed in Jesus Christ were captured in Kyoto, then the capital of Japan. Their ears were cut off to show people the cruel punishment others would undergo if they tried to become Catholics. Just before they were executed on the hill of Nagasaki, a soldier called to his side a young boy from among the captured, and asked him in public: "Listen, my boy, if you would give up your faith, I would make you a fine *samurai*. Now, you have a chance, so why don't you?" The lad said boldly: "I would prefer death to committing a grave sin and losing my soul."

The film gave me much food for thought. If Christians died for their faith, they really must have something to live by! They died willingly and triumphantly. They had something to die for. Their religion, then, should be something. I also thought of those missionaries who came all the way from Spain and died with those whom they baptized. Why did they leave their country, when they could have lived a happy married life at home?

The missionaries in the movie led me to think of two French Brothers on the campus. They, too, came all the way to Japan with a firm desire to die on our soil. By this time I was well acquainted with them; Brother Billman taught us English, and Brother Deiber taught us French. How often did I see them praying piously in the chapel! How did I know then that they were praying for me?

In the April of 1948, we welcomed a new principal, Brother Hisamatsu, and it is he who has influenced me more than anyone else. What amazed me was the fact that within a rather short period Brother Hisamatsu came to know each individual student by name. He had no particular class to teach, but seized every occasion to show interest in every one of the 800 students. Every morning we saw him standing at the school gate and saluting the students as they arrived. During recreation hours we took a walk with him. I myself thought that he was particularly interested in me, but later I found that many of my friends had the same impression about themselves in relation to Brother Hisamatsu. I saw in this man a living example of Jesus Christ as He said, "A new commandment I give you, that you love one another: that as I have loved you, you also love one another. By this will all men know that you are my disciples, if you have love for one another."

What impressed me most with regard to the Brothers was the fact that they lived a life of celibacy in order to dedicate their lives to God and men. They had no worldly property of their own; nevertheless, they were the happiest people in the world.

I have known quite a few wonderful Buddhists, but I have never seen any of them dedicating their lives so completely to the education of the youth. Strangely enough, while yet a non-Christian, I dreamed of becoming a religious and living a holy life set by their example.

In the spring of 1949, the four hundredth anniversary of St. Francis Xavier's arrival in Japan was celebrated in the Archdiocese of Osaka. I attended Mass at Nishinomiya Stadium and was deeply impressed by the great crowd that gathered there to praise God the Father.

On the following day the right hand of St. Francis was brought to the cathedral church for a public display, and I was privileged to witness it with my eyes. For the past four hundred years the saint's hand has been preserved incorrupt. It appeared to be living flesh. This amazed me a great deal, because there was no way of explaining such a phenomenon other than in terms of a miracle.

As I advanced in the knowledge of Christian doctrine through religion class, I came to convince myself of the divine origin of Christianity. While in Buddhism man seeks divinity, in Christianity God takes the initiative in revealing truth to us. In the former, man is compared to a perpetual traveler seeking truth; in the latter, on the contrary, divine truth has been already revealed to man so that he may accept it through faith. Certainly Buddhism teaches many good things about man, ethics, and human sufferings, but these good teachings are all contained in Christianity in an excellent manner. Moreover, Buddhism has nothing to say about the nature of God, and instead, lays emphasis on the illuminated soul. It also teaches us to nullify ourselves in order to attain a stage of union with the great soul permeating the universe, but the means to achieve this seem almost impossible to ordinary people. In Christianity, on the contrary, the purpose of man's life on earth is stated very clearly; it is to know, love, and serve God and finally to attain eternal happiness with God in heaven. Jesus Christ gave us a definite and visible means to achieve this; the Church and the seven Sacraments.

The more I came to know the Christian doctrine, the more firmly I came to convince myself of the absolute truth that the Catholic Church holds as divinely revealed. To be in both camps at the same time already seemed not only impossible but also contradictory and absurd. I said to myself: "Sooner or later I have to make up my mind."

I could hardly forget what Father Nakayama said rather casually in his religion class: "If you have just ten minutes a day to think about God, you are a happy man, but can you honestly say that you can't spare God ten minutes of your time? Spend, if not ten, five minutes to think of God, and you are still a happy man. If you don't have even five minutes, why don't you spend a minute a day to think about God, and you are still a happy man."

His words caught my full attention. They came back to my mind from time to time like a tide at the seashore. I then came to question who was this man to teach us a lesson like this. He was a Catholic priest, another Christ. I was certain that this man spent not just five or ten minutes a day, but hours in meditating about God every day.

My friend and I were very pleased when Father Nakayama explained to us about the new decree that came out of the bishops' council in Tokyo. He told us that it was not against Catholic faith, as decreed in the council, to show reverence at the home altar to honor the departed soul, since this was customary

and was an outward sign of respect for our dead
ancestors.

The Buddhists believe in heaven and hell. But
hell to them is not a place of eternal damnation.
Rather, it is a place for temporary satisfaction for
the sins committed, and every soul is eventually
transferred to heaven through the mercy of Buddha.
This appeared to be much more acceptable than the
Catholic teaching of hell as the place of eternal
punishment. However, when I came to consider
the effort that the Buddhists made to attain heaven,
I was somewhat disappointed. If everybody goes to
heaven eventually, why do we have to keep commandments? Why must we pursue perfection? The
only thing to do, then, is to throw ourselves on the
mercy of Buddha, and he will take care of us.
Isn't there something in life to live for? Life would
be worthless, if this were not true. It would hold
no purpose.

In the fall of 1950 I had an opportunity to attend a film that completely changed my thinking on
life and death. The movie was entitled "The Bells
of Nagasaki," and described the life of Doctor Nagai,
who was suffering from exposure as a result of the
atomic bomb. Doctor Nagai found his wife Midori
dead with her rosary in her hand. He rushed to see
his children, who were taken care of by his relatives.
One evening he knocked on the door of their house,
and his children immediately jumped out of bed
and clung to their father. The first question they
asked was: "Where is Mother, Dad?" The doctor
looked up heavenward slowly, and showing them the
rosary taken from his wife's hand, said: "Mother?
She is now in heaven."

They all cried, but I could never forget his
sincerity as he said firmly that his wife was in heaven.
Why did he not lose his mind when he found his

wife dead? Why did they take her death so beautifully? I immediately noticed that they had something to sustain their life firmly even in the midst of
tragedy. As I was riding alone on the train that
evening, I found myself already reaching the important decision, one which had been haunting me
for months. The tears came to my eyes, as I
thought of Doctor Nagai, a man of strong faith.
Like myself he had been a non-Christian, but was
received into the Catholic Church through the influence of his pious wife.

Day after day I prayed hard in the chapel so
that my parents would allow me to become a Catholic.
After all, I had been waiting for it for the past five
years. There was no doubt in my mind that
Catholicism was the only true religion. One day I
boldly asked my parents if I might be baptized. I
told them if they did not give their consent, I would
wait until I was twenty-one, at which time I would
need no permission. They were somewhat amazed
at my firm attitude and the consistency of my thought.
Finally, they allowed me to be baptized. How happy
was I to know that I would soon be received into
the Catholic Church!

The great day of my life finally arrived, December 8, 1951, the Feast of the Immaculate Conception
of the Blessed Virgin Mary. I was baptized by
Father Hisamatsu in the chapel. How deeply did
I thank God for the grace that he had bestowed upon
me! How happy I was when the Brothers and my
friends came to me and congratulated me for having
received the Sacrament of Baptism!

A year after my baptism, my mother was also
baptized on her death bed, and seven years later my
grandfather also received the same grace and went
to heaven. They all share in the holy sacrifice of
the Mass, as I offer it each morning.